SQL
Essentials

SQL
Essentials

by Richard Blum
and Allen G. Taylor

SQL Essentials For Dummies®

Published by: **John Wiley & Sons, Inc.**, 111 River Street, Hoboken, NJ 07030-5774, www.wiley.com

For general information on our other products and services, please contact our Customer Care Department within the U.S. at 877-762-2974, outside the U.S. at 317-572-3993, or fax 317-572-4002. For technical support, please visit https://hub.wiley.com/community/support/dummies.

Wiley publishes in a variety of print and electronic formats and by print-on-demand. Some material included with standard print versions of this book may not be included in e-books or in print-on-demand. If this book refers to media such as a CD or DVD that is not included in the version you purchased, you may download this material at http://booksupport.wiley.com. For more information about Wiley products, visit www.wiley.com.

Library of Congress Control Number: 2024948584

ISBN 978-1-394-29694-1 (pbk); ISBN 978-1-394-29696-5 (ebk); ISBN 978-1-394-29695-8 (ebk)

SKY10090206_110724

Contents at a Glance

Table of Contents

Introduction

SQL is the internationally recognized standard language for dealing with data in relational databases. Developed by IBM, SQL became an international standard in 1986. The standard was updated in 1989, 1992, 1999, 2003, 2008, 2011, 2016, and 2023. It continues to evolve and gain capability. Database vendors continually update their products to incorporate the new features of the ISO/IEC standard. (For the curious out there, ISO is the International Organization for Standardization, and IEC is the International Electrotechnical Commission.)

SQL isn't a general-purpose language, such as C++ or Java. Instead, it's strictly designed to deal with data in relational databases. With SQL, you can carry out all the following tasks:

>> Create a database, including all tables and relationships.

>> Fill database tables with data.

>> Change the data in database tables.

>> Delete data from database tables.

>> Retrieve specific information from database tables.

>> Grant and revoke access to database tables.

>> Protect database tables from corruption due to access conflicts or user mistakes.

About This Book

In this book, we cover how to use SQL to build and work with databases. Using SQL isn't just about knowing the terms and keywords, it's also about knowing when and how to use them to maximize performance of your application.

Here are some of the things you can do with this book:

>> Find out about the capabilities and limitations of SQL.

>> Discover how to develop reliable and maintainable database systems.

>> Create databases.

>> Speed database queries.

>> Control access to sensitive information.

Within this book, you may note that some web addresses break across two lines of text. If you're reading this book in print and want to visit one of these web pages, simply key in the web address exactly as it's noted in the text, pretending as though the line break doesn't exist. If you're reading this as an e-book, you've got it easy — just click the web address to be taken directly to the web page.

Foolish Assumptions

We know that this is a *For Dummies* book, but we don't really expect that you're a dummy. In fact, we assume that you're a very smart person. After all, you decided to read this book, which is a sign of high intelligence indeed. Therefore, we assume that you may want to do a few things, such as re-create some of the examples in the book. You may even want to enter some SQL code and execute it. To do that, you need at the very least an SQL editor and more likely also a relational database management system (RDBMS) of some sort. Many choices are available, both proprietary and open source. We mention several of these products at various places throughout the book but don't recommend any one in particular. Any product that complies with the ISO/IEC international SQL standard should be fine.

That said, take claims of ISO/IEC compliance with a grain of salt. No RDBMS available today is 100 percent compliant with the ISO/IEC SQL standard. For that reason, some of the code examples we give in this book may not work in the particular SQL implementation that you're using. The code samples we use in this book are consistent with the international standard rather than with the syntax of any particular implementation, unless we specifically state that the code is for a particular implementation.

Icons Used in This Book

For Dummies books are known for those helpful icons that point you in the direction of really great information. This section briefly describes the icons used in this book.

The Tip icon points out helpful information that's likely to make your job easier.

This icon marks a generally interesting and useful fact — something that you may want to remember for later use.

The Warning icon highlights lurking danger. When you see this icon, pay attention, and proceed with caution.

Where to Go from Here

If you're brand-new to the database world, start out in Chapter 1. It explains why databases are useful, and walks through a few of the different popular database software packages available.

If you're already familiar with database software packages, and you just want to dive into the nuts and bolts of working with databases, Chapters 2 through 5 cover all the things you'll need to know to get a database up and running.

If you're already an old hand at SQL and you want to dive into some more advanced topics, Chapters 6 through 8 cover the complicated world of database queries. There are plenty of ways to retrieve data from a database, but not all of them are efficient — especially if you have lots of data to work with!

Chapter 9 examines the dreaded security topic. If you're just creating a database for your own use, feel free to skip this chapter, but if you work in an environment where lots of people are going to need access to your database, this chapter is a must. Knowing how to protect your data from prying eyes has become a hot topic these days, and it's important to know just how to protect it.

Finally, Chapter 10 provides ten tips for improving your database experience when using SQL to retrieve data.

Chapter **1**

Getting to Know SQL

I n the early days of the relational database management system (RDBMS), there was no standard language for performing relational operations on data. A number of companies came out with RDBMS products, and each had its own associated language. However, differences in syntax and functionality made it impossible for a person using the language of one RDBMS to operate on data that had been stored by another. The creation of SQL solved this problem, but SQL is a continually evolving language that changes with each official release (the most recent being in 2023). This chapter explores just what SQL is (and isn't). It also takes a look at using SQL in some different database packages.

Knowing What SQL Does

SQL (pronounced *ess cue el*) is a software tool designed to deal with relational database data. It does far more than just execute queries. Yes, you can use it to retrieve the data you want from a database using a query. But you can also use SQL to create and destroy databases, as well as modify their structure. In addition, you can add, modify, and delete data with SQL. Even with all that capability, SQL is still considered only a *data sublanguage*, which means that it doesn't have all the features of general-purpose programming languages such as C, C++, C#, or Java.

SQL is specifically designed for dealing with relational databases, so it doesn't include a number of features needed for creating useful application programs. As a result, to create a complete application — one that handles queries, as well as provides access to a database — you have to write the code in one of the general-purpose languages and embed SQL statements within the program whenever it communicates with the database.

Knowing What SQL Does Not Do

Before we can tell you what SQL doesn't do, we need to give you some background information. In the 1930s, computer scientist and mathematician Alan Turing defined a very simple machine that could perform any computation that could be performed by any computer imaginable, regardless of how big and complex. This simple machine has come to be known as a *universal Turing machine*. Any computer that can be shown to be equivalent to a universal Turing machine is said to be *Turing-complete*. All modern computers are Turing-complete. Similarly, a computer language capable of expressing any possible computation is said to be Turing-complete. Practically all popular languages, including C, C#, C++, BASIC, FORTRAN, COBOL, Pascal, Java, and many others, are Turing-complete. SQL, however, is not.

Because standard SQL is not Turing-complete, you can't write an SQL program to perform a complex series of steps the way you can with a language such as C or Java. On the other hand, languages such as C and Java don't have the data-manipulation capabilities that SQL has, so you can't write a program with them that will efficiently operate on database data. There are several ways to solve this dilemma:

>> Combine the two types of language by embedding SQL statements within a program written in a host language such as C.

>> Have the C program make calls to SQL modules to perform data-manipulation functions.

>> Create a new language that includes SQL, but also incorporates those structures that would make the language Turing-complete. (This is essentially what Microsoft and Oracle have done with their versions of SQL.)

All three of these solutions are offered by various vendors.

Choosing and Using an Available RDBMS Implementation

SQL by itself isn't all that useful — you need a platform that stores the data itself and uses SQL to create, read, update, and delete (often called CRUD) the data. This is where the RDBMS comes in.

The RDBMS is a program that stores data in a manner that makes it easy to retrieve the data as quickly as possible. Storing data in a typical file isn't efficient, because in order to find a specific data item, the program would have to read through the entire file until it got to that data.

An RDBMS system uses various methods to store and index data so it can quickly find a specific data record, based on the SQL statement it's processing. There are plenty of different RDBMS programs available these days, each with different features to help increase data retrieval performance. In the following sections, we fill you in on some of the more common RDBMS programs available today.

Microsoft Access

Microsoft Access is an entry-level RDBMS with which developers can build relatively small and simple databases and database applications. It's designed for use by people with little or no training in database theory. You can build databases and database applications using Access, without ever seeing SQL. However, you can opt to use SQL in Access if you so choose.

Access runs under any of the Microsoft Windows operating systems, as well as Apple's macOS, but not under Linux or any other non-Microsoft operating system.

To reach the SQL editor in Access, do the following:

1. **Open a database that already has tables and at least one query defined.**

    A great place to start is with the Northwind Traders Starter Edition database provided as a free download with Access. The database includes a built-in mini-application that uses Access forms to help query and insert data. After you download the database, the application portion automatically starts, showing a form that asks you to create a user account for the application. After you log into the application, you see a database window that looks something like Figure 1-1, with the default Home tab visible. The icon at the left end of the Ribbon is the icon for Layout View, one of several available views. In this example, the pane on the left side of the window shows the different tables, forms, reports, queries, and scripts that have been created as part of the Northwind Traders Starter Edition database.

2. **Click the Queries entry in the pane on the left, and then double-click the qryProductOrders query.**

    The default view shows the data that's a result of the query.

3. **To see how the query is constructed, click the View icon at the top, and then select Design View.**

    The Design View for the query is shown in Figure 1-2. At the top is a graphical representation of the tables involved in the query, and below that is a list of the data fields that are retrieved in the query.

4. **Choose SQL View from the View drop-down menu.**

    Doing so shows the view displayed in Figure 1-3. It's the SQL code generated in order to display the result of the Team Membership of Paper Authors query.

    As you can see, it took a pretty complicated SQL statement to perform that Product Order query.

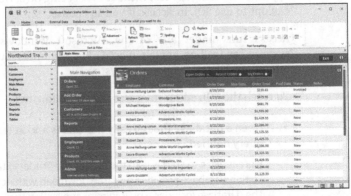

FIGURE 1-1: A Microsoft Access 365 database window running the Northwind Traders Starter Edition database.

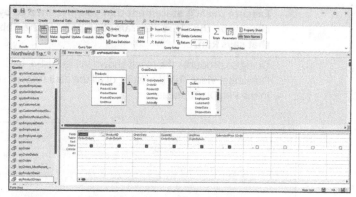

FIGURE 1-2: The Design view of the qryProductOrders query.

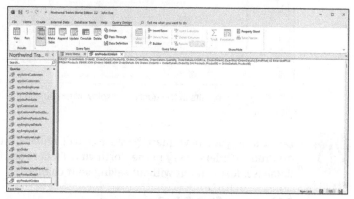

FIGURE 1-3: The SQL view of the qryProductOrders query.

When you're a true SQL master, you may want to enter a query directly using SQL, instead of going through the extra stage of using Access's QBE facility. When you get to the SQL Editor, which is where you are right now, you can do just that. Step 8 shows you how.

5. **Delete the SQL code currently in the SQL Editor pane and replace it with the query you want to execute.**

    For example, suppose you wanted to display all the rows and columns of the PRODUCTS table. The following SQL statement will do the trick:

    ```
    SELECT * FROM PRODUCTS ;
    ```

6. Execute the SQL statement that you just entered by clicking on the big red exclamation point in the ribbon that says Run.

Doing so produces the result shown in Figure 1-4, back in Datasheet View. This is a listing of all the data records stored in the PRODUCTS table.

FIGURE 1-4: The results of the query to display all the data in the PRODUCTS table.

WARNING

Don't save your new query because it will replace the standard qryProductOrders query in the Northwind Traders Starter Edition database. Just exit out without saving your changes.

Microsoft SQL Server

Microsoft SQL Server is Microsoft's entry into the enterprise database market. It runs only under one of the various Microsoft Windows operating systems. The latest version is SQL Server 2022. Unlike Microsoft Access, SQL Server requires a high level of expertise in order to use it at all. Users interact with SQL Server using Transact-SQL, also known as T-SQL. Additional functionality provides the developer with usability and performance advantages that Microsoft hopes will make SQL Server more attractive than its competitors. There is a free version of SQL Server 2022, called SQL Server 2022 Express Edition, that you may think of as SQL Server on training wheels. It's fully functional, but the size of database it can operate on is limited.

IBM DB2

IBM DB2 is a flexible product that runs on Windows and Linux PCs on the low end all the way up to IBM's largest mainframes. As you would expect for a DBMS that runs on big iron, it's a full-featured product. As with Microsoft's SQL Server, to use DB2 effectively, a developer must have received extensive training and considerable hands-on experience.

Oracle Database

Oracle Database is another DBMS that runs on PCs running the Windows, Linux, or macOS operating system, and also on very large, powerful computers.

SQL Developer is a free graphical tool that developers can use to enter and debug Oracle SQL code.

A free version of Oracle, called Oracle Database Express Edition, is available for download from the Oracle website (www.oracle.com/database/technologies/appdev/xe.html). It provides a convenient environment for learning Oracle. Migration to the full Oracle Database 11g product is smooth and easy when you're ready to move into production mode. The enterprise-class edition of Oracle hosts some of the largest databases in use today. (The same can be said for DB2 and SQL Server.)

Sybase SQL Anywhere

Sybase SQL Anywhere is a high-capacity, high-performance DBMS compatible with databases originally built with Microsoft SQL Server, IBM DB2, Oracle, and MySQL, as well as a wide variety of popular application-development languages. It features a self-tuning query optimizer and dynamic cache sizing.

REMEMBER

Tuning queries can make a big difference in their execution time. *Tuning* a query means making adjustments to it to make it run faster. *Dynamic cache sizing* means changing the size of the cache memory available to a query, based on the resources that the query needs to run as fast as possible. We talk about query tuning in Chapter 4.

MySQL

MySQL is the most widely used open-source DBMS. The defining feature of open-source software is that it's freely available to anyone. After downloading it, you can modify it to meet your needs and even redistribute it, as long as you give attribution to its source.

One amazing feature of MySQL is that it offers multiple ways of storing and managing data, which are called *storage engines*. The most feature-rich of these is the InnoDB storage engine, which provides many of the advanced database features found in commercial databases such as Microsoft SQL Server.

Another popular storage engine is the MyISAM storage engine, which is particularly noted for its speed. Although it lacks many of the advanced features found in the InnoDB storage engine, the MyISAM storage engine is amazingly fast with simple data queries, making it a popular choice for web-based applications. The MySQL server runs under Windows and Linux, but not under IBM's proprietary mainframe operating systems. MySQL is supported by a large and dedicated user community, which you can learn about at www.mysql.com.

PostgreSQL

PostgreSQL (pronounced *POST gress CUE el*) is another open-source DBMS, and it's generally considered to be more robust than MySQL, and more capable of supporting large enterprise-wide applications. It's also supported by an active user community. PostgreSQL runs under Linux, UNIX, Windows, and IBM's z/OS mainframe operating system.

IN THIS CHAPTER

» Building tables

» Setting constraints

» Establishing relationships between tables

» Altering table structure

» Deleting tables

Chapter **2**
Creating a Database with SQL

SQL is functionally divided into three components: the Data Definition Language (DDL), the Data Manipulation Language (DML), and the Data Control Language (DCL). The DDL consists of three statements: CREATE, ALTER, and DROP. You can use these statements to create database objects (such as tables), change the structure of an existing object, or delete an object. After you've designed a database, the first step in bringing it into reality is to build a table with the help of the DDL. After you've built the tables, the next step is to fill them with data. That's the job of the DML. As for the DCL, you call on it to help you preserve data integrity. In this chapter, we discuss the functions of the DDL.

First Things First: Planning Your Database

Before you can start constructing a database, you need to have a clear idea of the real-world or conceptual system that you're modeling. Some aspects of the system are of primary importance. Other aspects are subsidiary to the ones you've identified as primary. Additional aspects may not be important at all, depending on what you're using the database for. Based on these considerations, you'll build a model of the system based on the data entities and their relationships (called an *ER model*), with primary aspects identified as *entities* and subsidiary aspects identified as *attributes* of those entities. Unimportant aspects don't appear in the model at all.

After you've finalized your ER model, you can translate it into a normalized relational model. The relational model is your guide for creating database tables and establishing the relationships between them.

Building Tables

The fundamental object in a relational database is the table. Tables correspond directly to the relations in a normalized relational model. Table creation can be simple or quite involved. In either case, it's accomplished with a CREATE TABLE statement.

For our database example, let's imagine a local auto repair business located in the small town of Springfield, owned and operated by the fictional Abraham Hanks. Abe employs mechanics who perform repairs on the automobiles in the fleets of Abe's corporate customers. All of Abe's customers are corporations. Repair jobs are recorded in invoices, which include charges for parts and labor. Charges are itemized on separate lines on the invoices. The mechanics hold certifications in such specialty areas as brakes, transmissions, electrical systems, and engines. Abe buys parts from multiple suppliers. Multiple suppliers could potentially supply the same part.

Table 2-1 shows the tables (and their attributes) that correspond to the relational model we came up with for Ol' Honest Abe.

You can construct the DDL statements required to build the database tables directly from the enumeration of tables and columns in Table 2-1, but first you should understand the important topic of *keys*, which we discuss in the next section.

TABLE 2-1 **Tables for Honest Abe**

Table	Column
CUSTOMER	CustomerID
	CustomerName
	StreetAddr
	City
	State
	PostalCode
	ContactName
	ContactPhone
	ContactEmail
MECHANIC	EmployeeID
	FirstName
	LastName
	StreetAddr
	City
	State
	PostalCode
	JobTitle
CERTIFICATION	CertificationNo
	CertName
	Expires
INVOICE	InvoiceNo
	Date
	CustomerID
	EmployeeID
	Tax
	TotalCharge

(continued)

TABLE 2-1 *(continued)*

Table	Column
INVOICE_LINE	Invoice_Line_No
	PartNo
	UnitPrice
	Quantity
	Extended Price
	LaborChargeCode
LABOR	LaborChargeCode
	TaskDescription
	StandardCharge
PART	PartNo
	Name
	Description
	CostBasis
	ListPrice
	QuantityInStock
SUPPLIER	SupplierID
	SupplierName
	StreetAddr
	City
	State
	PostalCode
	ContactName
	ContactPhone
	ContactEmail
SUPPLIER_PART	SupplierID
	PartNo

Locating table rows with keys

Keys are the main tool used to locate specific rows within a table. Without a *key* — that handy item that guarantees that a row in a table is not a duplicate of any other row in the table — ambiguities can arise. The row you want to retrieve may be indistinguishable from one or more other rows in the table, meaning you wouldn't be able to tell which one was the right one.

There are several different terms you may see in discussions of keys that you can use to uniquely identify rows in a table:

» **Candidate key:** Ideally, at least one column or combination of columns within a table contains a unique entry in every row. Any such column or combination of columns is a candidate key. Perhaps your table has more than one such candidate. If your table has multiple candidate keys, select one of them to be the table's primary key.

» **The primary key:** A table's primary key has the characteristic of being a unique identifier of all the rows in the table. It's specifically chosen from among the candidate keys to serve as the primary identifier of table rows.

» **Composite key:** Sometimes no single column uniquely identifies every row in a table, but a combination of two or more columns does. Together, those columns comprise a composite key, which can collectively serve as a table's primary key.

Using the CREATE TABLE statement

When you understand the function of keys (see the preceding section), you can create tables using the CREATE TABLE statement. Whatever database development environment you're using will have a facility that enables you to enter SQL code. This is an alternative to using the form-based tools that the environment also provides. In general, it's a lot easier to use the provided form-based tool, but using SQL gives you the finest control over what you're doing.

```
CREATE TABLE CUSTOMER (
    CustomerID        INTEGER      PRIMARY KEY,
    CustomerName      CHAR (30),
```

```
        StreetAddr          CHAR (30),
        City                CHAR (25),
        State               CHAR (2),
        PostalCode          CHAR (10),
        ContactName         CHAR (30),
        ContactPhone        CHAR (13),
        ContactEmail        CHAR (30)) ;

CREATE TABLE MECHANIC (
        EmployeeID          INTEGER     PRIMARY KEY,
        FirstName           CHAR (15),
        LastName            CHAR (20),
        StreetAddr          CHAR (30),
        City                CHAR (25),
        State               CHAR (2),
        PostalCode          CHAR (10),
        JobTitle            CHAR (30)) ;

CREATE TABLE CERTIFICATION (
        CertificationNo     INTEGER     PRIMARY KEY,
        CertName            CHAR (30),
        Expires             Date) ;

CREATE TABLE INVOICE (
        InvoiceNo           INTEGER     PRIMARY KEY,
        Date                DATE,
        CustomerID          INTEGER,
        EmployeeID          INTEGER,
        Tax                 NUMERIC (9,2),
        TotalCharge         NUMERIC (9,2)) ;

CREATE TABLE INVOICE_LINE (
        Invoice_Line_No     INTEGER     PRIMARY KEY,
        PartNo              INTEGER,
        UnitPrice           NUMERIC (9,2),
        Quantity            INTEGER,
        ExtendedPrice       NUMERIC (9,2),
        LaborChargeCode     INTEGER) ;

CREATE TABLE LABOR (
        LaborChargeCode     INTEGER     PRIMARY KEY,
```

```
        TaskDescription      CHAR (40),
        StandardCharge       NUMERIC (9,2)) ;

CREATE TABLE PART (
        PartNo               INTEGER       PRIMARY KEY,
        Name                 CHAR (30),
        Description          CHAR (40),
        CostBasis            NUMERIC (9,2),
        ListPrice            NUMERIC (9,2),
        QuantityInStock      INTEGER) ;

CREATE TABLE SUPPLIER (
        SupplierID           INTEGER       PRIMARY KEY,
        SupplierName         CHAR (30),
        StreetAddr           CHAR (30),
        City                 CHAR (25),
        State                CHAR (2),
        PostalCode           CHAR (10),
        ContactName          CHAR (30),
        ContactPhone         CHAR (13),
        ContactEmail         CHAR (30)) ;

CREATE TABLE SUPPLIER_PART (
        SupplierID           INTEGER,
        PartNo               INTEGER,
        UNIQUE (SupplierID, PartNo)) ;
```

All the tables except SUPPLIER_PART have a single attribute
as their primary key. In the SUPPLIER_PART table, no single
attribute uniquely identifies a row, so the table has a composite
key made up of both SupplierID and PartNo. (That's the UNIQUE
(SupplierID, PartNo) business.) Those two attributes together
do uniquely identify each row in the table. Not all suppliers supply all parts, but there is a row in SUPPLIER_PART for every case
where a specific supplier supplies a specific part. The UNIQUE
constraint guarantees that no two rows in SUPPLIER_PART are
identical.

TIP

The data types used to define each of the data fields are discussed
in Chapter 3.

Setting Constraints

One way to protect the integrity of your data is to add constraints to your table definitions. There are several different kinds of constraints, including column constraints, table constraints, check constraints, and foreign key constraints. In this section, we cover column constraints and table constraints. Other types of constraints will pop up here and there in the book as we go along.

Column constraints

Column constraints determine what may or may not appear in a column of a table. For example, in the SUPPLIER_PART table, NOT NULL is a constraint on the SupplierID column. It guarantees that the SupplierID column must contain a value. It doesn't say what that value must be, as long as it is *some* value.

Table constraints

A table constraint is not restricted to a particular column but applies to an entire table. The PRIMARY KEY constraint is an example of a table constraint. A primary key may consist of one column, multiple columns, or even all the columns in the table — whatever it takes to uniquely identify every row in the table. Regardless of how many columns are included in the primary key, the primary key is a characteristic of the entire table.

Working with Keys and Indexes

Because primary keys uniquely identify each row in a table, they're ideal for indexes. The purpose of an index is to point to a row or set of rows that satisfies a condition. Because a primary key identifies one and only one row in a table, an index on a table's primary key provides the fastest, most direct access to the row it points to. Less selective indexes give access to multiple rows, all of which satisfy the selection condition. So, although CustomerID may take you directly to the record of the customer you want, you may not remember every customer's CustomerID. A search on LastName may return several records, but you can probably determine pretty quickly which one is the one you want. In such a case, you may want to create an index on the LastName column as well as on CustomerID. Any column that you frequently use as a retrieval condition should probably be indexed. If a table's primary key is a composite key, the index would be on the combination of all the columns that make up the key. Composite keys that are not a table's primary key can also be indexed. (We talk about creating primary keys in Chapter 3.)

Ensuring Data Validity with Domains

Although you, as a database creator, can't guarantee that the data entry operator always enters the correct data, at least you can ensure that the data entered is *valid* — that it excludes values that cannot possibly be correct. Do this with a CREATE DOMAIN statement. For example, in the LABOR table definition given in the earlier "Using the CREATE TABLE statement" section, the StandardCharge field holds currency values of the NUMERIC type. Suppose you want to ensure that a negative value is never entered for a StandardCharge. You can do so by creating a domain, as in the following example:

```
CREATE DOMAIN CurrencyDom NUMERIC (9,2)
    CHECK (VALUE >= 0);
```

You should now delete the old LABOR table and redefine it as shown below:

```
CREATE TABLE LABOR (
    LaborChargeCode    INTEGER       PRIMARY KEY,
    TaskDescription    CHAR (40),
    StandardCharge     CurrencyDom) ;
```

The data type of StandardCharge is replaced by the new domain. With a domain, you can constrain an attribute to assume only those values that are valid.

Establishing Relationships between Tables

After you've created tables for a database, the next step is to establish the relationships between the tables. A normalized relational database has multiple tables, perhaps hundreds of them.

Most queries or reports require data from more than one table. To pull the correct data from the tables, you must have a way of relating the rows in one table to corresponding rows in another table. This is accomplished with links consisting of columns in one table that correspond to columns in a related table.

Earlier in this chapter, we talk about primary keys and composite keys (which can be primary keys). Another important kind of key is the *foreign key*. Unlike primary keys, foreign keys do not uniquely identify a row in a table. Instead, they serve as links to other tables.

Relational databases are characterized by having multiple tables that are related to each other. Those relationships are established by columns that are shared between two tables. In a one-to-one relationship, one row in the first table corresponds to one and only one row in the second table. For a given row, one or more columns in the first table match a corresponding column or set of columns in the second table. In a one-to-many relationship, one row in the first table matches multiple rows in the second table. Once again, the match is made by columns in the first table that correspond to columns in the second table.

Consider the Honest Abe sample database in the "Building Tables" section, earlier in this chapter. It has a one-to-many link between CUSTOMER and INVOICE, mediated by the shared CustomerID column, and also a one-to-many link between MECHANIC and INVOICE mediated by the EmployeeID column. To create these links, you have to add a little more SQL code to the definition of the INVOICE table. Here's the new definition:

```
CREATE TABLE INVOICE (
    InvoiceNo           INTEGER      PRIMARY KEY,
    Date                DATE,
    CustomerID          INTEGER,
    EmployeeID          INTEGER,
    CONSTRAINT CustFK FOREIGN KEY (CustomerID)
        REFERENCES CUSTOMER (CustomerID),
    CONSTRAINT MechFK FOREIGN KEY (EmployeeID)
        REFERENCES MECHANIC (EmployeeID)
) ;
```

Adding the foreign key constraints to the table on the many side of a one-to-many relationship creates the links. For a one-to-one relationship, it doesn't matter which of the two tables you add the foreign key constraint to.

To tie the Honest Abe database together, add foreign key constraints to establish all the relationships. Here are the table definitions that would change with the foreign key constraints:

```
CREATE TABLE CERTIFICATION (
    CertificationNo    INTEGER       PRIMARY KEY,
    CertName           CHAR (30),
    MechanicID         INTEGER,
    Expires            Date,
    CONSTRAINT CertMechFK FOREIGN KEY (MechanicID)
        REFERENCES MECHANIC (EmployeeID)
) ;

CREATE TABLE INVOICE (
    InvoiceNo          INTEGER       PRIMARY KEY,
    Date               DATE,
    CustomerID         INTEGER,
    EmployeeID         INTEGER,
    Tax                NUMERIC (9,2),
    TotalCharge        NUMERIC (9,2),
    CONSTRAINT CustFK FOREIGN KEY (CustomerID)
        REFERENCES CUSTOMER (CustomerID),
    CONSTRAINT MechFK FOREIGN KEY (EmployeeID)
        REFERENCES MECHANIC (EmployeeID)
) ;

CREATE TABLE INVOICE_LINE (
    Invoice_Line_No    INTEGER       PRIMARY KEY,
    InvoiceNo          INTEGER,
    LaborChargeCode    INTEGER,
    PartNo             INTEGER,
    UnitPrice          NUMERIC (9,2),
    Quantity           INTEGER,
    ExtendedPrice      NUMERIC (9,2),
    LaborChargeCode    INTEGER,
    CONSTRAINT InvFK FOREIGN KEY (InvoiceNo)
        REFERENCES INVOICE (InvoiceNo),
```

```
    CONSTRAINT LaborFK FOREIGN KEY
      (LaborChargeCode)
          REFERENCES LABOR (LaborChargeCode),
    CONSTRAINT PartFK FOREIGN KEY (PartNo)
          REFERENCES PART (PartNo)
  ) ;

CREATE TABLE SUPPLIER_PART (
    SupplierID          INTEGER       NOT NULL,
    PartNo              INTEGER       NOT NULL,
    CONSTRAINT SuppFK FOREIGN KEY (SupplierID)
          REFERENCES SUPPLIER (SupplierID),
    CONSTRAINT PartSuppFK FOREIGN KEY (PartNo)
          REFERENCES PART (PartNo)
  ) ;
```

Foreign key constraints need to be added to only one side of a relationship. In a one-to-many relationship, they're added to the many side.

A database properly linked together using foreign keys is said to have *referential integrity*. The key to assuring referential integrity is to make sure that the ER diagram of the database is accurate and properly translated into a relational model, which is then converted into a relational database.

Altering Table Structure

In the real world, requirements tend to change. Sooner or later, this is bound to affect the databases that model some aspect of that world. SQL's DDL provides a means to change the structure of a database that has already been created. Structural changes can involve adding a new column to a table or deleting an existing one. The SQL to perform these tasks is pretty straightforward. Here's an example of adding a column:

```
ALTER TABLE MECHANIC
    ADD COLUMN Birthday DATE ;
```

Here's an example of deleting a column:

```
ALTER TABLE MECHANIC
    DROP COLUMN Birthday ;
```

Maybe Honest Abe decided not to keep track of employee birthdays after all.

Deleting Tables

It's just as easy to delete an entire table as it is to delete a column in a table. Here's how:

```
DROP TABLE CUSTOMER ;
```

Uh-oh. Be really careful about dropping tables. When it's gone, it's gone, along with all its data. Because of this danger, sometimes an RDBMS will not allow you to drop a table. If this happens, check to see whether a referential integrity constraint is preventing the drop operation. When two tables are linked with a primary key/foreign key relationship, you may be prevented from deleting the table on the primary key side, unless you first break that link by deleting the table on the foreign key side.

Chapter **3**

Drilling Down to the SQL Nitty-Gritty

n this chapter, we get into the nitty-gritty of SQL. You build a database to contain data, and it's important how you define that data to the database. As with many computer programming languages, SQL needs to define the type of data that the database is working with. In this chapter, we discuss the different data types defined in the SQL 2023 standard and how to work with them in database tables.

SQL's Data Types

SQL is capable of dealing with data of many different types — as this aptly named section will soon make clear. From the beginning, SQL has been able to handle the common types of numeric and character data, but more recently, new types have been added that enable SQL to deal with nontraditional data types, such as BLOB, CLOB, BINARY, and just recently added as part of SQL:2023, the JSON data type. At present, there are 13 major categories of data types:

» Exact numerics

» Approximate numerics

- Character strings
- Binary strings
- Booleans
- Datetimes
- Intervals
- XML
- ROW
- Collection
- REF
- JSON
- User-defined

Within each category, one or more specific types may exist.

REMEMBER

Your SQL implementation may not support all the data types that we describe in this section. Furthermore, your implementation may support nonstandard data types that we don't describe here.

With that proviso out of the way, read on to find brief descriptions of each of the categories, as well as enumerations of the standard types they include.

Exact numerics

Because computers store numbers in registers of finite size, there is a limit to how large or small a number can be and still be represented exactly. A range of numbers centered on zero can be represented exactly. The size of that range depends on the size of the registers that the numbers are stored in.

The next few sections drill down into each type.

INTEGER

Data of the INTEGER type is numeric data that has no fractional part. Any given implementation of SQL will have a limit to the number of digits that an integer can have. If, for some reason, you want to specify a maximum size for an integer that is less than the default maximum, you can restrict the maximum number of digits by specifying a *precision* argument.

SMALLINT

The SMALLINT data type is similar to the INTEGER type, but how it differs from the INTEGER type is implementation dependent. It may not differ from the INTEGER type at all. The only constraint on the SMALLINT type is that its precision may be no larger than the precision of the INTEGER type.

BIGINT

The BIGINT type is similar to the SMALLINT type. The only difference is that the precision of the BIGINT type can be no *smaller* than the precision of the INTEGER type. As is the case with SMALLINT, the precision of the BIGINT type could be the same as the precision of the INTEGER type.

NUMERIC

Data of the NUMERIC type *does* have a fractional part. This means the number contains a decimal point and zero or more digits to the right of the decimal point. For NUMERIC data, you can specify both precision and scale. The *scale* of a number is the number of digits to the right of the decimal point. For example, a variable declared as of type NUMERIC (10, 2) would have a maximum of ten digits, with two of those digits to the right of the decimal point.

DECIMAL

Data of the DECIMAL type is similar to data of the NUMERIC type with one difference: For data of the DECIMAL type, if the system you're running on happens to be able to handle numbers with more precision than what you've specified, the extra precision will be used.

TIP

The NUMERIC data type is better if portability is possible. When you use the NUMERIC type, you can be sure the precision you specify will be the precision that is used, regardless of the capabilities of the system. This ensures consistent results across diverse platforms.

DECFLOAT

DECFLOAT is an exact numeric data type in SQL:2016. It was added to ISO/IEC standard SQL specifically for business applications that deal with exact decimal values. Floating point data types, such as REAL and DOUBLE, can handle larger numbers than exact numerics such as NUMERIC and DECIMAL. However, they can't be counted upon to produce exact decimal values. DECFLOAT can handle larger numbers than other exact numeric data types and retain the exactness of an exact numeric type.

Approximate numerics

The approximate numeric types exist so that you can represent numbers either too large or too small to be represented by an exact numeric type.

REAL

The REAL data type is what you would normally use for single-precision floating-point numbers. The exact meaning of the term *single precision* depends on the implementation. This is hardware dependent. A machine with 64-bit registers will, in general, have a larger precision than a machine with 32-bit registers. How much larger may vary from one implementation to another.

DOUBLE PRECISION

A double-precision number, which is the basis for the DOUBLE data type, on any given system has greater precision than a real number on the same system. However, despite the name, a double-precision number does not necessarily have twice the precision of a real number. The most that can be said in general is that a double-precision number on any given system has greater precision than does a real number on the same system.

FLOAT

The FLOAT data type is very similar to the REAL data type. The difference is that with the FLOAT data type you can specify a precision. With the REAL and DOUBLE PRECISION data types, the default precision is your only option.

Character strings

After numbers, the next most common thing to be stored is strings of alphanumeric characters. SQL provides several character string types, each with somewhat different characteristics from the others, as described in the following sections.

CHARACTER

A column defined as being of type CHARACTER or CHAR can contain any of the normal alphanumeric characters of the language being used. A column definition also includes the maximum length allowed for an item of the CHAR type. Consider this example:

```
Name CHAR (15)
```

CHARACTER VARYING

The CHARACTER VARYING or VARCHAR data type is like the CHARACTER type in all respects except that short entries are not padded out with blanks to fill the field to the stated maximum.

```
Name VARCHAR (15)
```

TIP

The new SQL:2023 standard now allows you to define a VARCHAR data type without specifying the maximum length. In that case, the default maximum length allowed by the specific SQL implementation is used.

CHARACTER LARGE OBJECT

Any implementation of SQL has a limit to the number of characters that are allowed in a CHARACTER or CHARACTER VARYING field. If you want to store text that goes beyond that limit, you can use the CHARACTER LARGE OBJECT data type. The CLOB type, as it is affectionately known, is much less flexible than either the CHAR or VARCHAR types in that it does not allow you to do many of the fine-grained manipulations that you can do in those other types. You can compare two CLOB items for equality, but that's about all you can do.

NATIONAL CHARACTER, NATIONAL CHARACTER VARYING, and NATIONAL CHARACTER LARGE OBJECT

Different languages use different character sets. For example, Spanish and German have letters with diacritical marks that change the way the letter is pronounced. Other languages, such as Russian, have an entirely different character set. To store character strings that contain these different character sets, the various national character types have been added to SQL. If the English character type is the default on your system, as it is for most people, you can designate a different character set as your national character set. From that point on, when you specify a data type as NATIONAL CHARACTER, NATIONAL CHARACTER VARYING, or NATIONAL CHARACTER LARGE OBJECT, items in columns so specified use the chosen national character set rather than the default character set.

Binary strings

The various binary string data types were added to SQL:2008. Binary strings are like character strings except that the only characters allowed are 1 and 0. There are three different types of binary strings: BINARY, BINARY VARYING, and BINARY LARGE OBJECT.

BINARY

A string of binary characters of the BINARY type must be some multiple of 8 bits long. You can specify such a string with BINARY (x), where x is the number of bytes of binary data contained in the string. For example, if you specify a binary string with BINARY (2), then the string will be 2 bytes, or 16 bits, long. Byte one is defined as the first byte of the string.

BINARY VARYING

The BINARY VARYING or VARBINARY type is like the BINARY type except the string length doesn't need to be x bytes long. A string specified as VARBINARY (x) can be a minimum of zero bytes long and a maximum of x bytes long.

BINARY LARGE OBJECT

The BINARY LARGE OBJECT, or BLOB, type is used for a really large binary number. That large binary number may represent the pixels in a graphical image, or something else that doesn't seem to be a number. However, at the most fundamental level, it is a number.

Booleans

A column of the BOOLEAN data type, named after nineteenth-century English mathematician George Boole, will accept any one of three values: TRUE, FALSE, or UNKNOWN. The fact that SQL entertains the possibility of NULL values expands the traditional restriction of Boolean values from just TRUE and FALSE to TRUE, FALSE, and UNKNOWN. If a Boolean TRUE or FALSE value is compared to a NULL value, the result is UNKNOWN. Of course, comparing a Boolean UNKNOWN value to any value also gives an UNKNOWN result.

Datetimes

You often need to store either dates, times, or both, in addition to numeric and character data. ISO/IEC standard SQL defines five datetime types: DATE, TIME WITHOUT TIME ZONE, TIME WITH TIME ZONE, TIMESTAMP WITHOUT TIME ZONE, and TIMESTAMP WITH TIME ZONE.

TIP

Because considerable overlap exists among the five types, not all implementations of SQL include all five types. This could cause problems if you try to migrate a database from a platform that uses one subset of the five types to a platform that uses a different subset. There isn't much you can do about this except deal with it when the issue arises.

DATE

The DATE data type is the one to use if you care about the date of something but couldn't care less about the time of day within a date. The DATE data type stores a year, month, and day in that order, using ten character positions in the form yyyy-mm-dd. If you were recording the dates that humans first landed on the Moon, the entry for *Apollo 11* would be 1969-07-20.

TIME WITHOUT TIME ZONE

Suppose you want to store the time of day, but you don't care which day and, furthermore, you don't even care which time zone the time refers to? In that case, the TIME WITHOUT TIME ZONE data type is just the ticket. It stores hours, minutes, and seconds. The hours and minutes data occupies two digits apiece. The seconds data also occupies two digits, but in addition, it may include a fractional part for fractions of a second. If you specify a column as being of TIME WITHOUT TIME ZONE type, with no parameter, it will hold a time that has no fractional seconds. An example is 02:56:31, which is 56 minutes and 31 seconds after two o'clock in the morning.

For greater precision in storing a time value, you can use a parameter to specify the number of digits beyond the decimal point that will be stored for seconds. Here's an example of such a definition:

```
Smallstep TIME WITHOUT TIME ZONE (2),
```

In this example, there are two digits past the decimal point, so time is measured down to a hundredth of a second. It would take the form of 02:56:31.17.

TIME WITH TIME ZONE

The TIME WITH TIME ZONE data type gives you all the information that you get in the TIME WITHOUT TIME ZONE data type and adds the additional fact of what time zone the time refers to. All time zones around the Earth are referenced to Coordinated Universal Time (UTC), formerly known as Greenwich Mean Time (GMT). Coordinated Universal Time is the time in Greenwich, UK, which was the place where people first started being concerned with highly accurate timekeeping.

TIMESTAMP WITHOUT TIME ZONE

Just as sometimes you'll need to record dates and other times you'll need to record times, there will also be times when you need to store both times and dates. That's what the TIMESTAMP WITHOUT TIME ZONE data type is for. It's a combination of the DATE type and the TIME WITHOUT TIMEZONE type.

TIMESTAMP WITH TIME ZONE

If you have to record the time zone that a date and time refers to, use the TIMESTAMP WITH TIME ZONE data type. It's the same as the TIMSESTAMP WITHOUT TIME ZONE data type, with the addition of an offset that shows the time's relationship to UTC.

Intervals

An *interval* is the difference between two dates, two times, or two datetimes. There are two different kinds of intervals, the year-month interval and the day-hour-minute-second interval. A day always has 24 hours. An hour always has 60 minutes. A minute always has 60 seconds. However, a month may have 28, 29, 30, or 31 days. Because of that variability, you can't mix the two kinds of intervals.

XML

With the introduction of SQL/XML:2006, three specific subtypes of the XML type were defined: XML(SEQUENCE), XML(CONTENT), and XML(DOCUMENT). The three subtypes are related to each other hierarchically. An XML(SEQUENCE) is any sequence of XML nodes, XML values, or both. An XML(CONTENT) is an XML(SEQUENCE) that is an XML fragment wrapped in a document node. An XML(DOCUMENT) is an XML(CONTENT) that is a well-formed XML document.

ROW

The ROW type, introduced in the 1999 version of the ISO/IEC SQL standard (SQL:1999), represents the first break of SQL away from the relational model, as defined by its creator, Dr. E.F. Codd. With the introduction of this type, SQL databases can no longer be considered pure relational databases. One of the defining characteristics of Codd's First Normal Form (1NF) is the fact that no field in a table row may be multivalued. Multivalued fields are exactly what the ROW type introduces. The ROW type enables you to place a whole row's worth of data into a single field, effectively nesting a row within a row:

```
CREATE ROW TYPE address_type (
    Street      VARCHAR (25),
    City        VARCHAR (20),
    State       CHAR (2),
    PostalCode  VARCHAR (9) );
```

Collection

The introduction of ROW types in SQL:1999 was not the only break from the ironclad rules of relational database theory. In that same version of the standard, the ARRAY type was introduced, and in SQL:2003, the MULTISET type was added. Both of these collection types violate the ol' 1NF and, thus, take SQL databases a couple of steps farther away from relational purity.

ARRAY

The ARRAY type violates 1NF, but not in the same way that the ROW type does. The ARRAY type enables you to enhance a field of an existing type by putting more than one entry into it. This creates a repeating group, which was demonized in Codd's original formulation of the relational model but now reappears as a desirable feature. Arrays are ordered in the sense that each element in the array corresponds to exactly one ordinal position in the array.

```
CREATE TABLE VENDOR (
    VendorID    INTEGER             PRIMARY KEY,
```

```
VendorName   VARCHAR (25),
Address      address_type,
Phone        VARCHAR (15)  ARRAY [4] );
```

Multiset

Whereas an *array* is an ordered collection of elements, a *multiset* is an unordered collection. You can't reference individual elements in a multiset because you don't know where they're located in the collection. If you want to have multiples of an attribute, such as phone numbers, but you don't care what order they're listed in, you can use a multiset rather than an array.

REF

REF types are different from distinct data types such as INTEGER or CHAR. They're used in obscure circumstances by highly skilled SQL wizards, and just about nobody else. Instead of holding values, a REF type references a user-defined structured type associated with a typed table. Typed tables are beyond the scope of this book, but we mention REF types here for the sake of completeness.

REF types are not a part of core SQL. This means that database vendors can claim compliance with the SQL standard without implementing REF types.

JSON

The SQL:2016 standard introduced JavaScript Object Notation (JSON) operations, JSON data itself still had to be stored in character data type fields. The SQL:2023 standard adds a new JSON data type, specifically for storing JSON-formatted data. A JSON-formatted data value would look like this:

```
{
    "userid": "rblum",
    "name": "Richard Blum",
    "contact": "312-555-1234"
}
```

User-defined

User-defined types (UDTs) are another addition to SQL imported from the world of object-oriented programming. If the data types that we've enumerated here aren't enough for you, you can define your own data types. To do so, use the principles of abstract data types (ADTs) that are major features of such object-oriented languages as C++.

There are two kinds of UDTs: distinct types and structured types.

Distinct types

A *distinct* type is very similar to a regular predefined SQL type. In fact, a distinct type is derived directly from a predefined type, called the *source type*. You can create multiple distinct types from a single source type, each distinct from all the others and from the source type. Here's how to create a distinct type from a predefined type:

```
CREATE DISTINCT TYPE USdollar AS DECIMAL (10,2) ;
```

This definition (USdollar) creates a new data type for (wait for it) U.S. dollars, based on the predefined DECIMAL type. You can create additional distinct types in the same way:

```
CREATE DISTINCT TYPE Euro AS DECIMAL (10,2) ;
```

The USdollar type and the Euro type are both based on the DECIMAL type, but you can't directly compare a USdollar value to a Euro value, nor can you directly compare either of those to a DECIMAL value. This is consistent with reality because one U.S. dollar is not equal to one euro. However, it is possible to exchange dollars for euros and vice versa when traveling. You can make that exchange with SQL, too, but not directly. You must use a CAST operation, which we describe in Chapter 4.

Structured types

Structured types are not based on a single source type as are the distinct types. Instead, they're expressed as a list of attributes and methods. When you create a structured UDT, the relational database management system (RDBMS) automatically creates a constructor function, a mutator function, and an observer function. The *constructor* for a UDT is given the same name as the

UDT. Its job is to initialize the UDT's attributes to their default values. When you invoke a *mutator* function, it changes the value of an attribute of a structured type. You can then use an *observer* function to retrieve the value of an attribute of a structured type. If you include an observer function in a SELECT statement, it will retrieve values from the database.

Handling Null Values

A *null value* is a nonvalue. If you're talking about numeric data, a null value is not the same as zero, which is a definite value. It is one less than one. If you're talking about character data, a null value is not the same as a blank space. A blank space is also a definite value. If you're talking about Boolean data, a null value is not the same as FALSE. A false Boolean value is a definite value, too.

Applying Constraints

Constraints are one of the primary mechanisms for keeping the contents of a database from turning into a misleading or confusing mess. By applying constraints to tables, columns, or entire databases, you prevent the addition of invalid data or the deletion of data that is required to maintain overall consistency. A constraint can also identify invalid data that already exists in a database. If an operation that you perform in a transaction causes a constraint to be violated, the RDBMS will prevent the transaction from taking effect (being *committed*). This protects the database from being put into an inconsistent state.

Column constraints

You can constrain the contents of a table column. In some cases, that means constraining what the column *must* contain, and in other cases, what it may *not* contain. There are three kinds of column constraints: NOT NULL, UNIQUE, and CHECK.

NOT NULL

Although SQL allows a column to contain null values, there are times when you want to be sure that a column *always* has a distinct value. In order for one row in a table to be distinguished from another, there must be some way of telling them apart. This is usually done with a primary key, which must have a unique value in every row. Because a null value in a column could be anything, it may match the value for that column in any of the other rows. So, it makes sense to disallow a null value in the column that is used to distinguish one row from the rest. You can do this with a NOT NULL constraint, as shown in the following example:

```
CREATE TABLE CLIENT (

    ClientName      CHAR (30)      NOT NULL,
    Address1        CHAR (30),
    Address2        CHAR (30),
    City            CHAR (25),
    State           CHAR (2),
    PostalCode      CHAR (10),
    Phone           CHAR (13),
    Fax             CHAR (13),
    ContactPerson   CHAR (30)
    ) ;
```

When entering a new client into the CLIENT table, you must make an entry in the ClientName column.

UNIQUE

The NOT NULL constraint is a fairly weak constraint. You can satisfy the constraint as long as you put something into the field, even if what you put into the field would allow inconsistencies into your table.

For example, suppose you already had a client named David Taylor in your database, and someone tried to enter another record with the same client name. If the table were protected only by a NOT NULL constraint, the entry of the second David Taylor would be allowed. Now when you go to retrieve David Taylor's information, which one will you get? How will you know whether you have the one you want? A way around this problem is to use the stronger UNIQUE constraint.

TIP

Previous versions of the SQL standard were a little ambiguous on how the UNIQUE constraint handled NULL values, but the new SQL:2023 standard specifies that you can define the UNIQUE constraint to either allow duplicate NULL values or to disallow them by adding the DISTINCT clause.

CHECK

Use the CHECK constraint for preventing the entry of invalid data that goes beyond maintaining uniqueness. For example, you can check to make sure that a numeric value falls within an allowed range. You can also check to see that a particular character string is not entered into a column.

Here's an example that ensures that the charge for a service falls within the acceptable range. It ensures that a customer is not mistakenly given a credit rather than a debit, and that they are not charged a ridiculously high amount either.

```
CREATE TABLE TESTS (
    TestName          CHARACTER (30)        NOT NULL,
    StandardCharge    NUMERIC (6,2)
        CHECK (StandardCharge >= 0.00
            AND StandardCharge <= 200.00)
    ) ;
```

The constraint is satisfied only if the charge is positive and less than or equal to $200.

Table constraints

Sometimes a constraint applies not just to a column, but to an entire table. The PRIMARY KEY constraint is the principal example of a table constraint; it applies to an entire table.

Although a primary key *may* consist of a single column, it could also be made up of a combination of two or more columns. Because a primary key must be guaranteed to be unique, multiple columns may be needed if one column is not enough to guarantee uniqueness.

To see what we mean, check out the following, which shows a table with a single-column primary key:

```
CREATE TABLE PROSPECT (
    ProspectName    CHAR (30)      PRIMARY KEY,
    Address1        CHAR (30),
    Address2        CHAR (30),
    City            CHAR (25),
    State           CHAR (2),
```

```
PostalCode        CHAR (10),
Phone             CHAR (13),
Fax               CHAR (13)
) ;
```

The primary key constraint in this case is listed with the ProspectName column, but it is, nonetheless, a table constraint because it guarantees that the table contains no duplicate rows. By applying the primary key constraint to ProspectName, you're guaranteeing that ProspectName cannot have a null value, and no entry in the ProspectName column may duplicate another entry in the ProspectName column. Because ProspectName is guaranteed to be unique, every row in the table must be distinguishable from every other row.

ProspectName may not be a particularly good choice for a proposed primary key. Some people have rather common names— Joe Wilson or Jane Adams. It's quite possible that two people with the same name may both be prospects of your business. You could overcome that problem by using more than one column for the primary key. Here's one way to do that:

```
CREATE TABLE PROSPECT (
    ProspectName      CHAR (30)      NOT NULL,
    Address1          CHAR (30)      NOT NULL,
    Address2          CHAR (30),
    City              CHAR (25),
    State             CHAR (2),
    PostalCode        CHAR (10),
    Phone             CHAR (13),

    CONSTRAINT prospect_pk PRIMARY KEY
            (ProspectName, Address1)
    ) ;
```

A composite primary key is made up of both ProspectName and Address1.

TIP

Often you'll run into situations where the data fields don't lend themselves to providing unique values. Most database systems provide an autoincrement feature, which automatically assigns a unique key value to each data record.

Foreign key constraints

Relational databases are categorized the way they are because the data is stored in tables that are *related* to each other in some way. The relationship occurs because a row in one table may be directly related to one or more rows in another table.

For example, in a retail database, the record in the CUSTOMER table for customer Lisa Mazzone is directly related to the records in the INVOICE table for purchases that Ms. Mazzone has made. To establish this relationship, one or more columns in the CUSTOMER table must have corresponding columns in the INVOICE table.

The primary key of the CUSTOMER table uniquely identifies each customer. The primary key of the INVOICE table uniquely identifies each invoice. In addition, the primary key of the CUSTOMER table acts as a foreign key in INVOICE to link the two tables. In this setup, the foreign key in each row of the INVOICE table identifies the customer who made this particular purchase. Here's an example:

```
CREATE TABLE CUSTOMER (
      CustomerID          INTEGER        PRIMARY KEY,
      CustomerName        CHAR (30),
      Address1            CHAR (30),
      Address2            CHAR (30),
      City                CHAR (25),
      State               CHAR (2),
      PostalCode          CHAR (10),
      Phone               CHAR (13)
      ) ;
```

```
CREATE TABLE INVOICE (
      InvoiceNo           INTEGER        PRIMARY KEY,
      CustomerID          INTEGER,
      SalespersonID       INTEGER,

      CONSTRAINT customer_fk FOREIGN KEY (CustomerID)
            REFERENCES CUSTOMER (CustomerID),

      ) ;
```

Each invoice is related to the customer who made the purchase.

Assertions

Sometimes a constraint may apply not just to a column or a table, but to multiple tables or even an entire database. A constraint with such broad applicability is called an *assertion*.

Suppose a small bookstore wants to control its exposure to dead inventory by not allowing total inventory to grow beyond 20,000 items. Suppose further that stocks of books and DVDs are maintained in different tables — the BOOKS and DVD tables. An assertion can guarantee that the maximum is not exceeded.

```
CREATE TABLE BOOKS (
    ISBN        INTEGER,
    Title       CHAR (50),
    Quantity    INTEGER ) ;

CREATE TABLE DVD (
    BarCode     INTEGER,
    Title       CHAR (50),
    Quantity    INTEGER ) ;

CREATE ASSERTION
    CHECK ((SELECT SUM (Quantity)
            FROM BOOKS)
        + (SELECT SUM (Quantity)
            FROM DVD)
        < 20000) ;
```

This assertion adds up all the books in stock, adds up all the DVDs in stock, and finally adds those two sums together. It then checks to see that the sum of them all is less than 20,000. Whenever an attempt is made to add a book or DVD to inventory, and that addition would push total inventory to 20,000 or more, the assertion is violated and the addition is not allowed.

Operating on Data with the Data Manipulation Language

Just as the Data Definition Language (DDL) is the part of SQL that you can use to create or modify database structural elements such as schemas, tables, and views, the Data Manipulation Language

(DML) is the part of SQL that operates on the data that inhabits that structure.

There are four things that you want to do with data:

>> Store the data in a structured way that makes it easily retrievable.

>> Change the data that is stored.

>> Selectively retrieve information that responds to a need that you currently have.

>> Remove data from the database that is no longer needed.

SQL statements that are part of the DML enable you to do all these things. Adding, updating, and deleting data are all relatively straightforward operations. Retrieving the exact information you want out of the vast store of data not relevant to your current need can be more complicated. We give you only a quick look at retrieval here and go into more detail in Chapter 5. Here, we also tell you how to add, update, and delete data, as well as how to work with views.

Retrieving data from a database

The SQL SELECT statement is the primary tool for extracting whatever information you want from your database. Because the SELECT statement inquires about the contents of a table, it's called a *query*. A SELECT query can return all the data that a table contains, or it can be very discriminating and give you only what you specifically ask for. A SELECT query can also return selected results from multiple tables. We cover that in depth in Chapter 6.

In its simplest form, a SELECT statement returns all the data in all the rows and columns in whatever table you specify. Here's an example:

```
SELECT * FROM PRODUCT ;
```

The asterisk (*) is a wildcard character that means *everything*. In this context, it means return data from all the columns in the PRODUCT table. Because you're not placing any restrictions on which rows to return, all the data in all the rows of the table will be returned in the result set of the query.

There may be times when you want to see all the data in all the columns and all the rows in a table, but usually you're going to have a more specific question in mind. Perhaps you're not interested in seeing all the information about all the items in the PRODUCT table right now, but you're interested in seeing only the quantities in stock of all the guitars. You can restrict the result set that is returned by specifying the columns you want to see and by restricting the rows returned with a WHERE clause.

```
SELECT ProductID, ProductName, InStock
    FROM PRODUCT
    WHERE Category = 'guitar' ;
```

This statement returns the product ID number, product name, and number in stock of all products in the Guitar category, and nothing else. An ad hoc query such as this is a good way to get a quick answer to a question. Of course, there is a lot more to retrieving information than what we've covered briefly here. In Chapter 5, we have a lot more to say on the subject.

Adding data to a table

Somehow, you have to get data into your database. This data may be records of sales transactions, employee personnel records, instrument readings coming in from interplanetary spacecraft, or just about anything you care to keep track of. The form that the data is in determines how it is entered into the database. Naturally, if the data is on paper, you have to type it into the database. But if it's already in electronic form, you can translate it into a format acceptable to your RDBMS and then import it into your system. Either way, behind the scenes, you'll need to know how to use the INSERT statement.

Manually adding data

The dullest and most boring way to enter data into a database is to enter one record at a time, using SQL INSERT statements. It works, if you have no alternative way to enter the data, and all other methods of entering data ultimately are translated into SQL INSERT statements anyway. But after entering one or two records into the database this way, you'll probably have had enough. Here's an example of such an INSERT operation:

```
INSERT INTO CUSTOMER (CustomerID, FirstName,
    LastName, Street, City, State, Zipcode, Phone)
```

```
    VALUES (:vcustid, 'Abe', 'Lincoln',
 '1600 Pennsylvania Avenue NW', 'Washington', 'DC',
  '20500', '202-555-1414') ;
```

The first value listed, :vcustid, is a variable that is incremented each time a new record is added to the table. This guarantees that there will be no duplication of a value in the CustomerID field, which serves as the table's primary key.

REMEMBER

Single quotes enclose the values in the previous INSERT statement because the values are all of the CHAR type, which requires that values be enclosed in single quotes. INTEGER data, on the other hand, is not enclosed in single quotes. You might say, "Wait a minute! The zip code in the INSERT statement is an integer!" Well, no. It's only an integer if we define it as such when we create the CUSTOMER table. When we created this CUSTOMER table, CustomerID was the only column of the INTEGER type. All the rest are of the CHAR type. We're never going to want to add one zip code to another or subtract one from another, so there's no point in making them integers.

Adding incomplete records

Sometimes you may want to add a record to a table before you have data for all the record's columns. As long as you have the primary key and data for all the columns that have a NOT NULL or UNIQUE constraint, you can enter the record. Because SQL allows null values in other columns, you can enter such a partial record now and fill in the missing information later. Here's an example of how to do it:

```
INSERT INTO CUSTOMER (CustomerID, FirstName,
  LastName)
    VALUES (:vcustid, 'Abe', 'Lincoln') ;
```

Here you enter a new customer into the CUSTOMER table. All you have is the person's first and last name, but you can create a record in the CUSTOMER table anyway. The CustomerID is automatically generated and contained in the :vcustid variable. The value placed into the FirstName field is Abe and the value placed into the LastName field is Lincoln. The rest of the fields in this record will contain null values until you populate them at a later date.

REMEMBER

A NOT NULL constraint on a column raises a stink if you leave that particular column blank. A UNIQUE constraint gets similarly upset if you enter a value into a field that duplicates an already existing value in that same field (see the "Applying Constraints" section, earlier in this chapter).

Updating data in a table

The world in the twenty-first century is a pretty dynamic place. Things are changing constantly, particularly in areas that involve technology. Data that was of value last week may be irrelevant tomorrow. Facts that were inconsequential a year ago may be critically important now. For a database to be useful, it must be capable of rapid change to match the rapidly changing piece of the world that it models.

This means that, in addition to the ability to add new records to a database table, you also need to be able to update the records that it already contains. With SQL, you do this with an UPDATE statement. With an UPDATE statement, you can change a single row in a table, a set of rows that share one or more characteristics, or all the rows in the table. Here's the generalized syntax:

```
UPDATE table_name
    SET column_1 = expression_1 , column_2 =
    expression_2 ,
       ..., column_n = expression_n
    [WHERE predicates] ;
```

The SET clause specifies which columns will get new values and what those new values will be. The optional WHERE clause (square brackets indicate that the WHERE clause is optional) specifies which rows the update applies to. If there is no WHERE clause, the update is applied to all rows in the table.

For example, suppose that the cost of bike helmets increases to $22. You can make that change in the database with the following UPDATE statement:

```
UPDATE PRODUCT
    SET Cost = 22.00
    WHERE Name = 'Bike helmet' ;
```

This statement makes a change in all rows where Name is equal to Bike helmet.

TIP

If there is only one such row, only one is changed. If there is a possibility that more than one product may have the same name, you may erroneously update a row that you didn't intend, along with the one that you did. To avoid this problem, assuming you know the ProductID of the item you want to change, you should use the ProductID in your WHERE clause. In a well-designed database, ProductID would be the primary key and, thus, guaranteed to be unique.

```
UPDATE PRODUCT
    SET Cost = 22.00
    WHERE ProductID = 1664 ;
```

You may want to update a select group of rows in a table. To do that, you specify a condition in the WHERE clause of your update that applies to the rows you want to update and only the rows you want to update. For example, suppose management decides that the Helmets category should be renamed Headgear, to include hats and bandanas. Because their wish is your command, you duly change the category names of all the Helmet rows in the table to Headgear by doing the following:

```
UPDATE PRODUCT
    SET Category = 'Headgear'
    WHERE Category = 'Helmets' ;
```

Now suppose management decides it would be more efficient to lump headgear and gloves together into a single category named Accessories. Here's the UPDATE statement that will do that:

```
UPDATE PRODUCT SET Category = 'Accessories'
    WHERE Category = 'Headgear' OR Category =
    'Gloves' ;
```

All the headgear and gloves items are now considered accessories, but other categories, such as footwear, are left unaffected.

Now suppose management sees that considerable savings have been achieved by merging the headgear and gloves categories. The decision is made that the company is actually in the activewear business. To convert all company products to the new Activewear category, a really simple UPDATE statement will do the trick:

```
UPDATE PRODUCT
    SET Category = 'Activewear' ;
```

Deleting data from a table

If you no longer need data, get rid of it. With SQL, this is easy to do. First, decide whether you need to archive the data that you're about to delete, and save it in that location. After that's taken care of, deletion can be as simple as this:

```
DELETE FROM TRANSACTION
    WHERE TransDate < '2019-01-01' ;
```

Poof! All of 2018's transaction records are gone, and your database is speedy again. You can be as selective as you need to be with the WHERE clause and delete all the records you want to delete — and only the records you want to delete.

Chapter **4**

Values, Variables, Functions, and Expressions

This chapter describes the tools that ISO/IEC standard SQL:2023 provides to operate on data. In addition to specifying the value of a data item, you can slice and dice an item in a variety of ways. Instead of just retrieving raw data as it exists in the database, you can preprocess it to deliver just the information you want, in the form that you want it.

Entering Data Values

After you've created a database table, the next step is to enter data into it. SQL supports a number of different data types (see Chapter 3). Within any specific data type, the data can take any of several forms. Here are the five different forms that can appear in table rows:

» Row values

» Column references

>> Literal values

>> Variables

>> Special variables

Row values

A *row value* includes the values of all the data in all the columns in a row in a table. A row value is actually multiple values, not just one. The intersection of a row and a column, called a *field*, contains a single, so-called "atomic" value. All the values of all the fields in a row, taken together, are that single row's row value.

Column references

Just as you can specify a row value consisting of multiple values, you can specify the value contained in a single column. For illustration, consider this example from the Honest Abe database shown in Chapter 2:

```
SELECT * FROM CUSTOMER
    WHERE CustomerName = 'John Smith' ;
```

This query returns all the rows in the CUSTOMER table where the value in the CustomerName column is John Smith.

Literal values

In SQL, a value can be a constant or it can be represented by a variable. Constant values are called *literals*. Table 4-1 shows sample literals for each of the SQL data types.

TABLE 4-1 **Sample Literals of Various Data Types**

Data Type	Sample Literal
BIGINT	8589934592
INTEGER	186282
SMALLINT	186
NUMERIC	186282.42

Data Type	Sample Literal
DECIMAL	186282.42
DECFLOAT (16)	1234567890123456
REAL	6.02257E23
DOUBLE PRECISION	3.1415926535897E00
FLOAT	6.02257E23
BINARY (2)	'0110011111101010'
VARBINARY (1)	'10011'
CHARACTER(15)	'GREECE '
Note: Fifteen total characters and spaces are between the quote marks above.	
VARCHAR (CHARACTER VARYING)	'lepton'
NATIONAL CHARACTER(15)	'00395 ΛΛ00391Σ ' [1]
Note: Fifteen total characters and spaces are between the quote marks above.	
NATIONAL CHARACTER VARYING	'λεπτον' [2]
CHARACTER LARGE OBJECT (CLOB)	(A really long character string)
BINARY LARGE OBJECT (BLOB)	(A really long string of ones and zeros)
DATE	DATE '1969-07-20'
TIME(2)	TIME '13.41.32.50'
TIMESTAMP(0)	TIMESTAMP '2007-07-25-13.03.16.000000'
TIME WITH TIMEZONE(4)	TIME '13.41.32.5000-08.00'
TIMESTAMP WITH TIMEZONE(0)	TIMESTAMP '2007-07-25-13.03.16.0000+02.00'
INTERVAL DAY	INTERVAL '7' DAY

[1] This term is the word that Greeks use to name their own country in their own language. (The English equivalent is Hellas.)

[2] This term is the word lepton in Greek national characters.

Numeric literals are just the values that they represent. Nonnumeric literals are enclosed in single quotes.

The SQL:2023 standard adds a couple of new features to use with numeric literal values. For large integer values, you can add underscores to make the value more readable (for example, 1_000_000). You can also now specify nondecimal numeric literal values as binary, octal, or hexadecimal values. Binary values are preceded with 0b (for example, 0b1011), octal values with 0o (for example, 0o672), and hexadecimal values with 0x (for example, 0xA0FF).

Variables

Literals, which explicitly hold a single value, are fine if that value appears only once or twice in an application. However, if a value appears multiple times, and if there is any chance that value may change in the future, you should represent it with a variable. That way, if changes are necessary, you have to change the code in one place only, where the value is assigned to the variable, rather than in all the places in the application where that value appears.

For example, suppose an application dealing with a table containing the archives of a magazine retrieves information from various sections of the current issue. One such retrieval might look like this:

```
SELECT Editorial FROM PENGUINLIFE
    WHERE Issue = 47 ;
```

Another could be as follows:

```
SELECT LeadStory FROM PENGUINLIFE
    WHERE Issue = 47 ;
```

There could be many more like these two in the application. When next week rolls around and you want to run the application again for the latest issue, you must go through the program by hand and change all the instances of 47 to 48. Computers are supposed to rescue us from such boring, repetitive tasks, and they do. Instead of using literals in such cases, use variables instead, like this:

```
SET @IssueNumber = 48;
SELECT Editorial FROM PENGUINLIFE
```

```
      WHERE Issue = @IssueNumber ;
  SELECT LeadStory FROM PENGUINLIFE
      WHERE Issue = @IssueNumber ;
```

You have to change the IssueNumber variable in one place only, and the change affects all the places in the application where the variable appears.

Special variables

SQL has a few special variables that hold information about system usage. In multiuser systems, you often need to know who is using the system at any given time. This information can be captured in a log file, using one of the following special variables:

>> SESSION_USER: Holds a value that's equal to the user authorization identifier of the current SQL session. If you write a program that performs a monitoring function, you can interrogate SESSION_USER to find out who is executing SQL statements.

>> CURRENT_USER: Stores a user-specified authorization identifier. If a module has no such identifier, CURRENT_USER has the same value as SESSION_USER.

>> SYSTEM_USER: Contains the operating system's user identifier. This identifier may differ from that user's identifier in an SQL module. A user may log onto the system as ANDREW, for example, but identify himself to a module as DIRECTOR. The value in SESSION_USER is DIRECTOR. If the user makes no explicit specification of the module identifier, and CURRENT_USER also contains DIRECTOR, SYSTEM_USER holds the value ANDREW.

One use of the SYSTEM_USER, SESSION_USER, and CURRENT_USER special variables is to track who is using the system. You can maintain a log table and periodically insert into that table the values that SYSTEM_USER, SESSION_USER, and CURRENT_USER contain. The following example shows how:

```
INSERT INTO USAGELOG (SNAPSHOT)
    VALUES ('User ' || SYSTEM_USER ||
        ' with ID ' || SESSION_USER ||
        ' active at ' || CURRENT_TIMESTAMP) ;
```

This statement produces log entries similar to the following example:

```
User ANDREW with ID DIRECTOR active at
2019-01-03-23.50.00
```

Working with Functions

Functions perform computations or operations that are more elaborate than what you would expect a simple command statement to do. SQL has two kinds of functions: set functions and value functions. *Set functions* are so named because they operate on a set of rows in a table rather than on a single row. *Value functions* operate on the values of fields in a table row.

Summarizing data with set functions

When dealing with a set of table rows, often what you want to know is some aggregate property that applies to the whole set. SQL has five such aggregate or set functions: COUNT, AVG, MAX, MIN, and SUM. To see how these work, consider the example data for a table named PAPERS in Table 4-2. It's a price table for photographic papers of various sizes and characteristics.

TABLE 4-2 **Photographic Paper Price List per 20 Sheets**

Paper Type	Size8	Size11
Dual-sided matte	8.49	13.99
Card stock dual-sided matte	9.49	16.95
Professional photo gloss	10.99	19.99
Glossy HW 9M	8.99	13.99
Smooth silk	10.99	19.95
Royal satin	10.99	19.95
Dual-sided semigloss	9.99	17.95
Dual-sided HW semigloss	—	—
Universal two-sided matte	—	—
Transparency	29.95	—

The fields that contain dashes do not have a value. The dash in the table represents a null value.

COUNT

The COUNT function returns the number of rows in a table, or the number of rows that meet a specified condition. In the simplest case, you have

```
SELECT COUNT (*)
   FROM PAPERS ;
```

This returns a value of 10 because there are ten rows in the PAPERS table. You can add a condition to see how many types of paper are available in Size 8:

```
SELECT COUNT (Size8)
   FROM PAPERS ;
```

This returns a value of 8 because, of the ten types of paper in the PAPERS table, only eight are available in size 8. You may also want to know how many different prices there are for papers of size 8. That is also easy to determine:

```
SELECT COUNT (DISTINCT Size8)
   FROM PAPERS ;
```

This returns a value of 6 because there are six distinct values of Size 8 paper. Null values are ignored.

AVG

The AVG function calculates and returns the average of the values in the specified column. It works only on columns that contain numeric data.

```
SELECT AVG (Size8)
   FROM PAPERS ;
```

This returns a value of 12.485. If you wonder what the average price is for the Size 11 papers, you can find out this way:

```
SELECT AVG (Size11)
   FROM PAPERS ;
```

This returns a value of 17.539.

MAX

As you may expect, the MAX function returns the maximum value found in the specified column. Find the maximum value in the Size8 column:

```
SELECT MAX (Size8)
   FROM PAPERS ;
```

This returns 29.95, the price for 20 sheets of Size 8 transparencies.

MIN

The MIN function gives you the minimum value found in the specified column.

```
SELECT MIN (Size8)
   FROM PAPERS ;
```

Here the value returned is 8.49.

SUM

In the case of the photographic paper example, it doesn't make much sense to calculate the sum of all the prices for the papers being offered for sale, but in other applications, this type of calculation can be valuable. Just in case you want to know what it would cost to buy 20 sheets of every Size 11 paper being offered, you could make the following query:

```
SELECT SUM (Size11)
   FROM PAPERS ;
```

It would cost 122.77 to buy 20 sheets of each of the seven kinds of Size 11 paper that are available.

LISTAGG

LISTAGG is a set function, defined in the SQL:2016 ISO/IEC specification. Its purpose is to transform the values from a group of rows into a list of values delimited by a character that doesn't occur within the data. An example would be to transform a group of table rows into a string of comma-separated values (CSVs).

```
SELECT LISTAGG(LastName, ', ')
        WITHIN GROUP (ORDER BY LastName)
   "Customer"
   FROM CUSTOMER
   WHERE Zipcode = 97201;
```

This statement will return a list of all customers residing in the 97201 zip code, in ascending order of their last names. This will work as long as there are no commas in the LastName field of any customer.

ANY_VALUE

The ANY_VALUE function, new in SQL:2023, returns any non-null value from the specified data set.

```
SELECT ANY_VALUE(Size8)
   FROM PAPERS;
```

This function will return a randomly selected value from the data values stored in the Size8 column of the data records.

Dissecting data with value functions

A number of data manipulation operations occur fairly frequently. SQL provides value functions to perform these tasks. There are four types of value functions:

>> String

>> Numeric

>> Datetime

>> Interval

In the following subsections, we look at the functions available in each of these categories.

String value functions

String value functions take one character string as input and produce another character string as output. There are 12 string value functions, as described in this section.

SUBSTRING (FROM)

The operation of SUBSTRING (FROM) is similar to substring operations in many other computer languages. Here's an example:

```
SUBSTRING ('manual transmission' FROM 8 FOR 4)
```

This returns tran, the substring that starts in the eighth character position and continues for four characters. You want to make sure that the starting point and substring length you specify locate the substring entirely within the source string. If part or all of the substring falls outside the source string, you could receive a result you aren't expecting.

REMEMBER

Some implementations do not adhere strictly to the ANSI/ISO standard syntax for the SUBSTRING function, or for the other functions that follow. Check the documentation of the implementation you're using if the code samples given here don't work for you.

SUBSTRING (SIMILAR)

SUBSTRING (SIMILAR) is a regular expression substring function. It divides a string into three parts and returns the middle part. Formally, a regular expression is a string of legal characters. A substring is a particular designated part of that string. Consider this example:

```
SUBSTRING ('antidisestablishmentarianism'
          SIMILAR 'antidis\"[:ALPHA:]+\"arianism'
          ESCAPE '\')
```

The original string is the first operand. The operand following the SIMILAR keyword is a character string literal that includes a regular expression in the form of another character string literal, a separator (\"), a second regular expression that means "one or more alphabetic characters," a second separator (\"), and a third regular expression in the form of a different character string literal. The value returned is

```
establishment
```

UPPER

The UPPER function converts its target string to all uppercase.

```
UPPER ('ChAoTic')                    returns 'CHAOTIC'
```

The UPPER function has no effect on character sets, such as Hebrew, that do not distinguish between uppercase and lowercase.

LOWER

The LOWER function converts its target string to all lowercase.

```
LOWER ('INTRUDER ALERT!') returns
   'intruder alert!'
```

As is the case for UPPER, LOWER has no effect on character sets that do not include the concept of case.

TRIM

In the SQL:2023 standard, the TRIM function enables you to crop a string, shaving off one character at the front or the back of the string — or both. Here are a few examples:

```
TRIM (LEADING ' ' FROM ' ALERT ')
   returns 'ALERT '
TRIM (TRAILING ' ' FROM ' ALERT ')
   returns ' ALERT'
TRIM (BOTH ' ' FROM ' ALERT ')
   returns 'ALERT'
TRIM (LEADING 'A' FROM 'ALERT')
   returns 'LERT'
```

If you don't specify what to trim, the blank space (' ') is the default.

WARNING

Many current SQL implementations don't follow this standard behavior for the TRIM function. Instead, the TRIM function they implement behaves similar to the new LTRIM and RTRIM functions (described in the following section).

LTRIM AND RTRIM

Because of the disparate behavior of the TRIM function implemented by various database packages, the SQL:2023 standard tries to accommodate the different implementations by adding the LTRIM and RTRIM functions. These functions expand on the standard TRIM function by allowing you to shave off multiple instances of the specified character left (LTRIM) or right (RTRIM) of the specified string.

```
LTRIM('    ALERT ', ' ')        returns 'ALERT '
RTRIM(' ALERT      ', ' ')      returns ' ALERT'
```

As with the TRIM function, if you don't specify what to trim, the blank space (' ') is the default.

TIP

Unfortunately, there is no function for trimming multiple characters off of both the left *and* right sides of the string. To do that, you'll need to use both functions on the same string.

LPAD AND RPAD

The SQL:2023 standard adds the LPAD and RPAD functions, which allow you to pad a string value to a specific size.

```
LPAD('Rich', 10, ' ')       returns '      Rich'
RPAD('Rich', 10, ' ')       returns 'Rich      '
```

As with the TRIM function, if you don't specify what to pad, the padding character is the blank space (' ') by default.

TRANSLATE AND CONVERT

The TRANSLATE and CONVERT functions take a source string in one character set and transform the original string into a string in another character set. Examples may be Greek to English or Katakana to Norwegian. The conversion functions that specify these transformations are implementation specific, so we don't give any details here.

These functions don't really translate character strings from one language to another. All they do is translate a character from the first character set to the corresponding character in the second character set. In going from Greek to English, it would convert 00395λλασ to Ellas instead of translating it as Greece. ("00395λλασ" is what the Greeks call their country. We have no idea why English speakers call it Greece.)

OVERLAY

The OVERLAY function is a SUBSTRING function with a little extra functionality. As with SUBSTRING, it finds a specified substring within a target string. However, instead of returning the string that it finds, it replaces it with a different string. For example:

```
OVERLAY ('I Love Paris' PLACING 'Tokyo' FROM 8 FOR
5)
```

This changes the string to

```
I Love Tokyo
```

This won't work if you want to change I Love Paris to I Love London. The number of letters in London does not match the number of letters in Paris.

Numeric value functions

Numeric value functions can take a variety of data types as input, but the output is always a numeric value. SQL has 16 types of numeric value functions. The defining characteristic of a function is that it returns a value of some sort. Numeric value functions always return a numeric value. Thus, the square root function will return a value that is the square root of the input; the natural logarithm function will return a value that is the natural logarithm of the input, and so on.

POSITION

POSITION searches for a specified target string within a specified source string and returns the character position where the target string begins. The syntax is as follows:

```
POSITION (target IN source)
```

Table 4-3 shows a few examples.

If the function doesn't find the target string, the POSITION function returns a zero value. If the target string has zero length (as in the last example), the POSITION function always returns a value of 1. If any operand in the function has a null value, the result is a null value.

TABLE 4-3 **Sample Uses of the POSITION Statement**

This Statement	Returns
POSITION ('T' IN 'Transmission, automatic')	1
POSITION ('Tra' IN 'Transmission, automatic')	1
POSITION ('au' IN 'Transmission, automatic')	15
POSITION ('man' IN 'Transmission, automatic')	0
POSITION (' ' IN 'Transmission, automatic')	1

EXTRACT

The EXTRACT function extracts a single field from a datetime or an interval. The following statement, for example, returns 12:

```
EXTRACT (MONTH FROM DATE '2018-12-04')
```

CHARACTER_LENGTH

The CHARACTER_LENGTH function returns the number of characters in a character string. The following statement, for example, returns 20:

```
CHARACTER_LENGTH ('Transmission, manual')
```

REMEMBER

As you can see, commas and even blank spaces count as characters. Note that this function is not particularly useful if its argument is a literal like 'Transmission, manual'. You can write 20 just as easily as you can write CHARACTER_LENGTH ('Transmission, manual'). In fact, writing 20 is easier. This function is more useful if its argument is an expression rather than a literal value.

OCTET_LENGTH

In music, a vocal ensemble made up of eight singers is called an *octet*. Typically, the parts that the ensemble represents are first and second soprano, first and second alto, first and second tenor, and first and second bass. In computer terminology, an ensemble of eight data bits is called a *byte*. The word *byte* is clever in that the term clearly relates to *bit* but implies something larger than a bit. A nice wordplay — but unfortunately, nothing in the word *byte* conveys the concept of "eightness." By borrowing the musical term, a more apt description of a collection of eight bits becomes possible.

Practically all modern computers use eight bits to represent a single alphanumeric character. More complex character sets (such as Chinese) require 16 bits to represent a single character. The OCTET_LENGTH function counts and returns the number of octets (bytes) in a string. If the string is a bit string, OCTET_LENGTH returns the number of octets you need to hold that number of bits. If the string is an English-language character string (with one octet per character), the function returns the number of characters in the string. If the string is a Chinese character string, the function returns a number that is twice the number of Chinese characters. The following string is an example:

```
OCTET_LENGTH ('Brakes, disc')
```

This function returns 12 because each character takes up one octet.

Some character sets use a variable number of octets for different characters. In particular, some character sets that support mixtures of Kanji and Latin characters use *escape* characters to switch between the two character sets. A string that contains both Latin and Kanji may have, for example, 30 characters and require 30 octets if all the characters are Latin; 62 characters if all the characters are Kanji (60 characters plus a leading and trailing shift character); and 150 characters if the characters alternate between Latin and Kanji (because each Kanji character needs two octets for the character and one octet each for the leading and trailing shift characters). The OCTET_LENGTH function returns the number of octets you need for the current value of the string.

CARDINALITY

Cardinality deals with collections of elements such as arrays or multisets, where each element is a value of some data type. The cardinality of the collection is the number of elements that it contains. One use of the CARDINALITY function is something like this:

```
CARDINALITY (TeamRoster)
```

This function would return 12, for example, if there were 12 team members on the roster. TeamRoster, a column in the TEAM table, can be either an array or a multiset. An *array* is an ordered collection of elements, and a *multiset* is an unordered collection of elements. For a team roster, which changes frequently, a multiset makes more sense. (You can find out more about arrays and multisets in Chapter 3.)

ABS

The ABS function returns the absolute value of a numeric value expression.

```
ABS (-273)
```

This returns 273.

TRIGONOMETRIC FUNCTIONS SIN, COS, TAN, ASIN, ACOS, ATAN, SINH, COSH, TANH

The trig functions give you the values you would expect, such as the sine of an angle or the hyperbolic tangent of one.

LOGARITHMIC FUNCTIONS LOG10, LN, LOG (<BASE>, <VALUE>)

The logarithmic functions enable you to generate the logarithm of a number, either a base-10 logarithm, a natural logarithm, or a logarithm to a base that you specify.

MOD

The MOD function returns the *modulus* — the remainder of division of one number by another — of two numeric value expressions.

```
MOD (6,4)
```

This function returns 2, the modulus of six divided by four.

EXP

This function raises the base of the natural logarithms *e* to the power specified by a numeric value expression:

```
EXP (2)
```

This function returns something like 7.389056. The number of digits beyond the decimal point is implementation dependent.

POWER

This function raises the value of the first numeric value expression to the power of the second numeric value expression:

```
POWER (3,7)
```

This function returns 2187, which is 3 raised to the seventh power.

SQRT

This function returns the square root of the value of the numeric value expression:

```
SQRT (9)
```

This function returns 3, the square root of 9.

FLOOR

This function rounds the numeric value expression to the largest integer not greater than the expression:

```
FLOOR (2.73)
```

This function returns 2.0.

CEIL OR CEILING

This function rounds the numeric value expression to the smallest integer not less than the expression.

```
CEIL (2.73)
```

This function returns 3.0.

GREATEST

Because the set functions already use the MAX function, the SQL:2023 standard defines the GREATEST function to use for numeric values.

```
GREATEST(1.0,2.0,3.5)
```

This functions returns 3.5.

LEAST

Because the set functions already use the `MIN` function, the SQL:2023 standard defines the `LEAST` function to use for numeric values.

```
LEAST(1.0, 2.0, 3.5)
```

This function returns 1.0.

WIDTH_BUCKET

The `WIDTH_BUCKET` function, used in online application processing (OLAP), is a function of four arguments, returning an integer between the value of the second (minimum) argument and the value of the third (maximum) argument. It assigns the first argument to an equiwidth partitioning of the range of numbers between the second and third arguments. Values outside this range are assigned to either the value of zero or one more than the fourth argument (the number of buckets). For example:

```
WIDTH_BUCKET (PI, 0, 10, 5)
```

Suppose `PI` is a numeric value expression with a value of 3.141592. The example partitions the interval from 0 to 10 into five equal *buckets*, each with a width of 2. The function returns a value of 2 because 3.141592 falls into the second bucket, which covers the range from 2 to 4.

Datetime value functions

SQL includes three functions that return information about the current date, current time, or both. `CURRENT_DATE` returns the current date, `CURRENT_TIME` returns the current time, and `CURRENT_TIMESTAMP` returns both the current date and the current time. `CURRENT_DATE` doesn't take an argument, but `CURRENT_TIME` and `CURRENT_TIMESTAMP` both take a single argument. The argument specifies the precision for the seconds part of the time value that the function returns. Datetime data types and the precision concept are described in Chapter 3.

The following table offers some examples of these datetime value functions.

This Statement	Returns
CURRENT_DATE	2019-01-23
CURRENT_TIME (1)	08:36:57.3
CURRENT_TIMESTAMP (2)	2019-01-23 08:36:57.38

The date that CURRENT_DATE returns is DATE type data. The time that CURRENT_TIME (*p*) returns is TIME type data, and the timestamp that CURRENT_TIMESTAMP (*p*) returns is TIMESTAMP type data. The precision (*p*) specified is the number of digits beyond the decimal point, showing fractions of a second. Because SQL retrieves date and time information from your computer's system clock, the information is correct for the time zone in which the computer resides.

In some applications, you may want to deal with dates, times, or timestamps as character strings to take advantage of the functions that operate on character data. You can perform a type conversion by using the CAST expression, which we describe later in this chapter.

Polymorphic table functions

A table function is a user-defined function that returns a table as a result. A polymorphic table function, first described in SQL:2016, is a table function whose row type is not declared when the function is created. Instead, the row type may depend on the function arguments used when the function is invoked.

Using Expressions

An *expression* is any combination of elements that reduces to a single value. The elements can be numbers, strings, dates, times, intervals, Booleans, or more complex things. What they are doesn't matter, as long as after all operations have taken place, the result is a single value.

Numeric value expressions

The operands in a numeric value expression can be numbers of an exact numeric type or of an approximate numeric type. (Exact and approximate numeric types are discussed in Chapter 3.) Operands of different types can be used within a single expression. If at least one operand is of an approximate type, the result is of an approximate type. If all operands are of exact types, the result is of an exact type. The SQL specification does not specify exactly what type the result of any given expression will be, due to the wide variety of platforms that SQL runs on.

Here are some examples of valid numeric value expressions:

» -24

» 13 + 78

» 4 * (5 + 8)

» Weight / (Length * Width * Height)

» Miles / 5280

String value expressions

String value expressions can consist of a single string or a concatenation of strings. The concatenation operator (||) joins two strings together and is the only one you can use in a string value expression. Table 4-4 shows some examples of string value expressions and the strings that they produce.

TABLE 4-4   Examples of String Value Expressions

String Value Expression	Resulting String
'nanotechnology'	'nanotechnology'
'nano' || 'technology'	'nanotechnology'
'nano' || ' ' || 'technology'	'nanotechnology'
'Isaac' || ' ' || 'Newton'	'Isaac Newton'
FirstName || ' ' || LastName	'Isaac Newton'
B'10101010' || B'01010101'	B'1010101001010101'

From the first two rows in Table 4-4, you see that concatenating two strings produces a result string that has seamlessly joined the two original strings. The third row shows that concatenating a null value with two source strings produces the same result as if the null were not there. The fourth row shows concatenation of two strings while retaining a blank space in between. The fifth row shows the concatenation of two variables with a blank space in between and produces a string consisting of the values of those variables separated by a blank space. Finally, the last line of Table 4-4 shows the concatenation of two binary strings; the result is a single binary string that is a seamless combination of the two source strings.

Datetime value expressions

Datetime value expressions perform operations on dates and times. Such data is of the DATE, TIME, TIMESTAMP, or INTERVAL type. The result of a datetime value expression is always of the DATE, TIME, or TIMESTAMP type. Intervals are not one of the datetime types, but an interval can be added to or subtracted from a datetime to produce another datetime. Here's an example datetime value expression that makes use of an added interval:

```
CURRENT_DATE + INTERVAL '2' DAY
```

This expression evaluates to the day after tomorrow.

Datetimes can also include time zone information. The system maintains times in Coordinated Universal Time (UTC), previously known as Greenwich Mean Time (GMT). You can specify a time as being either at your local time or as an offset from UTC. An example is

```
TIME '13:15:00' AT LOCAL
```

for 1:15 p.m. local time. Another example is

```
TIME '13:15:00' AT TIME ZONE INTERVAL '-8:00'
    HOUR TO MINUTE
```

for 1:15 p.m. Pacific Standard Time. (Pacific Standard Time is eight hours earlier than UTC.)

Interval value expressions

An *interval* is the difference between two datetimes. If you subtract one datetime from another, the result is an interval. It makes no sense to add two datetimes, so SQL doesn't allow you to do it.

There are two kinds of intervals: year-month and day-time. This situation is a little messy, but it's necessary because not all months contain the same number of days. A month can be 28, 29, 30, or 31 days long, so there is no direct translation from days to months. As a result, when using an interval, you must specify which kind of interval it is. Suppose you expect to take an around-the-world cruise after you retire, starting on June 1, 2045. How many years and months is that from now? An interval value expression gives you the answer:

```
(DATE '2045-06-01' - CURRENT_DATE) YEAR TO MONTH
```

You can add two intervals to obtain an interval result:

```
INTERVAL '30' DAY + INTERVAL '14' DAY
```

However, you cannot do the following:

```
INTERVAL '30' DAY + INTERVAL '14' MONTH
```

The two kinds of intervals don't mix. Besides addition and subtraction, multiplication and division of intervals also are allowed. The expression

```
INTERVAL '7' DAY * 3
```

is valid and gives an interval of 21 days. The expression

```
INTERVAL '12' MONTH / 2
```

is also valid and gives an interval of 6 months. Intervals can also be negative.

```
INTERVAL '-3' DAY
```

gives an interval of −3 days. Aside from the literals we use in the previous examples, any value expression or combination of value expressions that evaluates to an interval can be used in an interval value expression.

Boolean value expressions

Only three legal Boolean values exist: TRUE, FALSE, and UNKNOWN. The UNKNOWN value becomes operative when a NULL is involved.

Suppose the Boolean variable `Signal1` is TRUE and the Boolean variable `Signal2` is FALSE. The following Boolean value expression evaluates to TRUE:

```
Signal1 IS TRUE
```

So does this one:

```
Signal1 IS TRUE OR Signal2 IS TRUE
```

However, the following Boolean value expression evaluates to FALSE.

```
Signal1 IS TRUE AND Signal2 IS TRUE
```

The AND operator means that both predicates must be true for the result to be true. (A *predicate* is an expression that asserts a fact about values.) Because `Signal2` is false, the entire expression evaluates to a FALSE value.

Array value expressions

You can use a couple of types of expressions with arrays. The first has to do with cardinality. The maximum number of elements an array can have is called the array's *maximum cardinality*. The actual number of elements in the array at a given time is called its *actual cardinality*. You can combine two arrays by concatenating them, summing their maximum cardinalities in the process. Suppose you want to know the actual cardinality of the concatenation of two array-type columns in a table, where the first element of the first column has a given value. You can execute the following statement:

```
SELECT CARDINALITY (FirstColumn || SecondColumn)
   FROM TARGETTABLE
WHERE FirstColumn[1] = 42 ;
```

The CARDINALITY function gives the combined cardinality of the two arrays, where the first element in the first array has a value of 42.

Note: The first element of an SQL array is considered to be element 1, rather than element 0 as is true for some other languages.

Conditional value expressions

The value of a conditional value expression depends on a condition. SQL offers three variants of conditional value expressions: CASE, NULLIF, and COALESCE.

Handling different cases

The CASE conditional expression was added to SQL to give it some of the functionality that all full-featured computer languages have, the ability to do one thing if a condition holds and another thing if the condition does not hold. Originally conceived as a data sublanguage that was concerned only with managing data, SQL has gradually gained features that enable it to take on more of the functions needed by application programs.

SQL actually has two different CASE structures: the CASE expression described here, and a CASE statement. The CASE expression, like all expressions, evaluates to a single value. You can use a CASE expression anywhere where a value is legal. The CASE statement, on the other hand, doesn't evaluate to a value. Instead, it executes a block of statements.

The CASE expression searches a table, one row at a time, taking on the value of a specified result whenever one of a list of conditions is TRUE. If the first condition is not satisfied for a row, the second condition is tested, and if it is TRUE, the result specified for it is given to the expression, and so on until all conditions are processed. If no match is found, the expression takes on a NULL value. Processing then moves to the next row.

SEARCHING FOR TABLE ROWS THAT SATISFY VARIOUS CONDITIONS

You can specify the value to be given to a CASE expression, based on which of several conditions is satisfied. Here's the syntax:

```
CASE
    WHEN condition1 THEN result1
    WHEN condition2 THEN result2
    ...
    WHEN conditionN THEN resultN
    ELSE resultx
END
```

If, in searching a table, the CASE expression finds a row where condition1 is true, it takes on the value of result1. If condition1 is not true, but condition2 is true, it takes on the value of result2. This continues for all conditions. If none of the conditions is met and there is no ELSE clause, the expression is given the NULL value. Here's an example of usage:

```
UPDATE MECHANIC
    Set JobTitle = CASE
                         WHEN Specialty = 'Brakes'
                                    THEN 'Brake Fixer'
                         WHEN Specialty = 'Engines'
                                    THEN 'Motor Master'
                         WHEN Specialty =
    'Electrical'
                                    THEN 'Wizard'
                         ELSE 'Apprentice'
                     END ;
```

THE EQUALITY CONDITION ALLOWS A COMPACT CASE VALUE EXPRESSION

A shorthand version of the CASE statement can be used when the condition, as in the previous example, is based on one thing being equal (=) to one other thing. The syntax is as follows:

```
CASE valuet
    WHEN value1 THEN result1
    WHEN value2 THEN result2
    ...
    WHEN valueN THEN resultN
    ELSE resultx
END
```

For the preceding example, this translates to

```
UPDATE MECHANIC
    Set JobTitle = CASE Specialty
                    WHEN 'Brakes' THEN 'Brake Fixer'
                    WHEN 'Engines' THEN 'Motor Master'
                    WHEN 'Electrical' THEN 'Wizard'
                             ELSE 'Apprentice'
        END ;
```

If the condition involves anything other than equality, the first, nonabbreviated form must be used.

The NULLIF special CASE

SQL databases are unusual in that NULL values are allowed. A NULL value can represent an unknown value, a known value that just hasn't been entered into the database yet, or a value that doesn't exist. Most other languages that deal with data don't support nulls, so whenever a situation arises in such databases where a value is not known, not yet entered, or nonexistent, the space is filled with a value that would not otherwise occur, such as –1 in a field that never holds a negative value, or ∗∗∗ in a character field in which asterisks are not valid characters.

To migrate data from a database that does not support nulls to an SQL database that does, you can use a CASE statement such as the following:

```
UPDATE MECHANIC
    SET Specialty = CASE Specialty
                        WHEN '***' THEN NULL
                        ELSE Specialty
                    END ;
```

You can do the same thing in a shorthand manner, using a NULLIF expression, as follows:

```
UPDATE MECHANIC
    SET Specialty = NULLIF(Specialty, '***') ;
```

Admittedly, this looks more cryptic than the CASE version, but it does save some tedious typing. You could interpret it as, "Update the MECHANIC table by setting the value of Specialty to NULL if its current value is '∗∗∗'."

Bypassing null values with COALESCE

The COALESCE expression is another shorthand version of CASE that deals with NULL values. It examines a series of values in a table row and assumes the value of the first one that is not NULL. If all the listed values are NULL, the COALESCE expression takes on the NULL value. Here's the syntax for a CASE expression that does this:

```
CASE
    WHEN value1 IS NOT NULL
         THEN value1
    WHEN value2 IS NOT NULL
         THEN value2
    ...
    WHEN valueN is NOT NULL
         THEN valueN
    ELSE NULL
END
```

Here's the syntax for the equivalent COALESCE expression:

```
COALESCE(value1, value2, ..., valueN)
```

If you're dealing with a large number of cases, the COALESCE version can save you quite a bit of typing.

Converting data types with a CAST expression

In Chapter 3, we describe the data types that SQL recognizes. The host languages in which SQL statements are often embedded also recognize data types, and those host language data types are never an exact match for the SQL data types. This could present a problem, except for the fact that, with a CAST expression, you can convert data of one type into data of another type. Whereas the first type may not be compatible with the place you want to send the data, the second type is. Of course, not all conversions are possible. If you have a character string such as '2019-02-14', you can convert it to the DATE type with a CAST expression. However, SQL doesn't let you convert a character string such as 'rhinoceros' to the DATE type. The data to be converted must be compatible with the destination type.

For example, suppose you have a table named ENGINEERS with a column named SSN, which is of the NUMERIC type. Perhaps you have another table, named MANAGERS, that has a column named SocSecNo, which is of the CHAR (9) type. A typical entry in SSN might be 987654321. To find all the engineers who are also managers, you can use the following query. The CAST expression converts the CHAR (9) type to the NUMERIC type so that the operation can proceed.

```
SELECT * FROM ENGINEER
    WHERE ENGINEER.SSN = CAST(MANAGER.SocSecNo
    AS INTEGER) ;
```

This returns all the rows from the ENGINEER table that have
Social Security numbers that match Social Security numbers in
the MANAGERS table. To do so, it changes the Social Security
number from the MANAGER table from the CHAR (9) type to the
INTEGER type, for the purposes of the comparison.

Row value expressions

Row value expressions (as distinct from mere row values, which
are covered at the beginning of this chapter) enable you to deal
with the data in an entire table row or a subset of a row. The
other expressions that we've shown deal only with a single field
in a row at a time. Row value expressions are useful for adding
new data to a table a row at a time, or to specify the retrieval of
multiple fields from a table row. Here's an example of a row value
expression used to enter a new row of data to a table:

```
INSERT INTO CERTIFICATIONS
    (CertificationNo, CertName,
    MechanicID, Expires)
    VALUES
    (1, 'V8 Engines', 34, 2021-07-31) ;
```

One advantage of using row value expressions is that many SQL
implementations can process them faster than the equivalent
one-field-at-a-time operations. This could make a significant
difference in performance at runtime.

Chapter **5**

SELECT Statements and Modifying Clauses

The main purpose of storing data on a computer is to be able to retrieve specific elements of the data when you need them. As databases grow in size, the proportion that you're likely to want on any given occasion becomes smaller. As a result, SQL provides tools that enable you to make retrievals in a variety of ways. With these tools — SELECT statements and modifying clauses — you can zero in on the precise pieces of information that you want, even though they may be buried among megabytes of data that you're not interested in at the moment.

Finding Needles in Haystacks with the SELECT Statement

SQL's primary tool for retrieving information from a database is the SELECT statement. In its simplest form, with one modifying clause (a FROM clause), it retrieves everything from a table. By adding more modifying clauses, you can whittle down what it retrieves until you're getting exactly what you want, no more and no less.

Suppose you want to display a complete list of all the customers in your CUSTOMER table, including every piece of data that the table stores about each one. That is the simplest retrieval you can do. Here's the syntax:

```
SELECT * FROM CUSTOMER ;
```

The asterisk (*) is a wildcard character that means *all columns*. This statement returns all the data held in all the rows of the CUSTOMER table. Sometimes that is exactly what you want. Other times, you may want only *some* of the data on *some* of the customers — those who satisfy one or more conditions. For such refined retrievals, you must use one or more modifying clauses.

WARNING

Returning more data fields than you actually need may sound trivial, but it can drastically decrease the performance of a query. It's usually best to avoid using the asterisk unless you really do use all the data.

Modifying Clauses

In any SELECT statement, the FROM clause is mandatory. You *must* specify the source of the data you want to retrieve. Other modifying clauses are optional. They serve several different functions:

>> The WHERE clause specifies a condition. Only those table rows that satisfy the condition are returned.

>> The GROUP BY clause rearranges the order of the rows returned by placing rows together that have the same value in a grouping column.

>> The HAVING clause filters out groups that do not meet a specified condition.

>> The ORDER BY clause sorts whatever is left after all the other modifying clauses have had a chance to operate.

The next few sections look at these clauses in greater detail.

FROM clauses

The FROM clause is easy to understand if you specify only one table, as in the previous example.

```
SELECT * FROM CUSTOMER ;
```

This statement returns all the data in all the rows of every column in the CUSTOMER table. You can, however, specify more than one table in a FROM clause. Consider the following example:

```
SELECT *
  FROM CUSTOMER, INVOICE ;
```

This statement forms a virtual table that combines the data from the CUSTOMER table with the data from the INVOICE table. Each row in the CUSTOMER table combines with every row in the INVOICE table to form the new table. The new virtual table that this combination forms contains the number of rows in the CUSTOMER table multiplied by the number of rows in the INVOICE table. If the CUSTOMER table has 10 rows and the INVOICE table has 100, the new virtual table has 1,000 rows.

This operation is called the *Cartesian product* of the two source tables. The Cartesian product is a type of JOIN. We cover JOIN operations in detail in Chapter 7.

In most applications, the majority of the rows that form as a result of taking the Cartesian product of two tables are meaningless. In the case of the virtual table that forms from the CUSTOMER and INVOICE tables, only the rows where the CustomerID from the CUSTOMER table matches the CustomerID from the INVOICE table would be of any real interest. You can filter out the rest of the rows by using a WHERE clause.

Row pattern recognition is a new capability that was added to the FROM clause in SQL:2016. It enables you to find patterns in a data set. The capability is particularly useful in finding patterns in time series data, such as stock market quotes or any other data set where it would be helpful to know when a trend reverses direction. The row pattern recognition operation is accomplished with a MATCH_RECOGNIZE clause within an SQL statement's FROM clause. The syntax of the row pattern recognition operation is more complex than we want to get into in this overview of modifying clauses. It's described in detail in ISO/IEC TR 19075-5:2016(E), Section 3, which is available for free from ISO. As of this writing, of the major relational database management system (RDBMS) products, only Oracle implements row pattern recognition.

WHERE clauses

We use the WHERE clause many times throughout this book without really explaining it because its meaning and use are obvious: A statement performs an operation (such as a SELECT, DELETE, or UPDATE) only on table rows where a stated condition is TRUE. The syntax of the WHERE clause is as follows:

```
SELECT column_list
    FROM table_name
    WHERE condition ;

DELETE FROM table_name
    WHERE condition ;

UPDATE table_name
    SET column₁ =value₁ , column₂ =value₂ ,
    ..., column_n =value_n
    WHERE condition ;
```

The condition in the WHERE clause may be simple or arbitrarily complex. You may join multiple conditions together by using the logical connectives AND, OR, and NOT (which we discuss later in this chapter) to create a single condition.

The following statements show you some typical examples of WHERE clauses:

```
WHERE CUSTOMER.CustomerID = INVOICE.CustomerID
WHERE MECHANIC.EmployeeID =
    CERTIFICATION.MechanicID
WHERE PART.QuantityInStock < 10
WHERE PART.QuantityInStock > 100
    AND PART.CostBasis > 100.00
```

The conditions that these WHERE clauses express are known as predicates. A *predicate* is an expression that asserts a fact about values.

The predicate PART.QuantityInStock < 10, for example, is True if the value for the current row of the column PART.QuantityInStock is less than 10. If the assertion is True, it satisfies the condition. An assertion may be True, False, or UNKNOWN.

The UNKNOWN case arises if one or more elements in the assertion are null. The *comparison predicates* (=, <, >, <>, <=, and >=) are the most common, but SQL offers several others that greatly increase your capability to distinguish, or filter out, a desired data item from others in the same column. Here are the predicates that give you that filtering capability:

>> Comparison predicates

>> BETWEEN

>> IN and NOT IN

>> LIKE and NOT LIKE

>> NULL

>> ALL, SOME, and ANY

>> EXISTS

>> UNIQUE

>> DISTINCT

>> OVERLAPS

>> MATCH

The mechanics of filtering can get a bit complicated, so in the following sections we explain the mechanics of each predicate.

Comparison predicates

The examples in the preceding section show typical uses of comparison predicates in which you compare one value to another. For every row in which the comparison evaluates to a True value, that value satisfies the WHERE clause, and the operation (SELECT, UPDATE, DELETE, or whatever) executes upon that row. Rows that the comparison evaluates to FALSE are skipped. Consider the following SQL statement:

```
SELECT * FROM PART
   WHERE QuantityInStock < 10 ;
```

This statement displays all rows from the PART table that have a value of less than 10 in the QuantityInStock column.

Six comparison predicates are listed in Table 5-1.

TABLE 5-1 SQL's Comparison Predicates

Comparison	Symbol
Equal	=
Not equal	<>
Less than	<
Less than or equal	<=
Greater than	>
Greater than or equal	>=

BETWEEN

Sometimes you want to select a row if the value in a column falls within a specified range. One way to make this selection is by using comparison predicates. For example, you can formulate a WHERE clause to select all the rows in the PART table that have a value in the QuantityInStock column greater than 10 and less than 100, as follows:

```
WHERE PART.QuantityInStock > 10 AND
    PART.QuantityInStock < 100
```

This comparison doesn't include parts with a quantity in stock of exactly 10 or 100 — only those values that fall in between these two numbers. To include the end points, you can write the statement as follows:

```
WHERE PART.QuantityInStock >= 10 AND
    PART.QuantityInStock <= 100
```

Another (potentially simpler) way of specifying a range that includes the end points is to use a BETWEEN predicate, like this:

```
WHERE PART.QuantityInStock BETWEEN 10 AND 100
```

This clause is functionally identical to the preceding example, which uses comparison predicates. This formulation saves some typing and is a little more intuitive than the one that uses two comparison predicates joined by the logical connective AND.

WARNING

The BETWEEN keyword may be confusing because it doesn't tell you explicitly whether the clause includes the end points. In fact, the clause *does* include these end points. BETWEEN also fails to tell you explicitly that the first term in the comparison must be equal to or less than the second. If, for example, PART.QuantityInStock contains a value of 50, the following clause returns a TRUE value:

```
WHERE PART.QuantityInStock BETWEEN 10 AND 100
```

However, a clause that you may think is equivalent to the preceding example returns the opposite result, False:

```
WHERE PART.QuantityInStock BETWEEN 100 AND 10
```

REMEMBER

If you use BETWEEN, you must be able to guarantee that the first term in your comparison is always equal to or less than the second term.

You can use the BETWEEN predicate with character, bit, and date-time data types, as well as with the numeric types. You may see something like the following example:

```
SELECT FirstName, LastName
   FROM CUSTOMER
   WHERE CUSTOMER.LastName
      BETWEEN 'A' AND 'Mzzz' ;
```

This example returns all customers whose last names are in the first half of the alphabet.

IN and NOT IN

The IN and NOT IN predicates deal with whether specified values (such as GA, AL, and MS) are contained within a particular set of values (such as the states of the United States). You may, for example, have a table that lists suppliers of a commodity that your company purchases on a regular basis. You want to know the phone numbers of those suppliers located in the southern United States. You can find these numbers by using comparison predicates, such as those shown in the following example:

```
SELECT Company, Phone
   FROM SUPPLIER
```

```
WHERE State = 'GA' OR State = 'AL'
    OR State = 'MS' ;
```

You can also use the IN predicate to perform the same task, as follows:

```
SELECT Company, Phone
    FROM SUPPLIER
    WHERE State IN ('GA', 'AL', 'MS') ;
```

This formulation is more compact than the one using comparison predicates and logical OR.

The NOT IN version of this predicate works the same way. Say that you have locations in New York, New Jersey, and Connecticut, and to avoid paying sales tax, you want to consider using suppliers located anywhere except in those states. Use the following construction:

```
SELECT Company, Phone
    FROM SUPPLIER
    WHERE State NOT IN ('NY', 'NJ', 'CT') ;
```

Using the IN keyword this way saves you a little typing. Saving a little typing, however, isn't that great an advantage. You can do the same job by using comparison predicates, as shown in this section's first example.

TIP

You may have another good reason to use the IN predicate rather than comparison predicates, even if using IN doesn't save much typing. Your RDBMS probably implements the two methods differently, and one of the methods may be significantly faster than the other on your system. You may want to run a performance comparison on the two ways of expressing inclusion in (or exclusion from) a group and then use the technique that produces the quicker result. An RDBMS with a good optimizer will probably choose the more efficient method, regardless of which kind of predicate you use. A performance comparison gives you some idea of how good your RDBMS's optimizer is. If a significant difference between the run times of the two statements exists, the quality of your RDBMS's optimizer is called into question.

The IN keyword is valuable in another area, too. If IN is part of a subquery, the keyword enables you to pull information from two tables to obtain results that you can't derive from a single table. We cover subqueries in detail in Chapter 6, but following is an example that shows how a subquery uses the IN keyword.

Suppose that you want to display the names of all customers who've bought the flux capacitor product in the last 30 days. Customer names are in the CUSTOMER table, and sales transaction data is in the PART table. You can use the following query:

```
SELECT FirstName, LastName
  FROM CUSTOMER
  WHERE CustomerID IN
    (SELECT CustomerID
      FROM INVOICE
      WHERE SalesDate >= (CurrentDate - 30)
        AND InvoiceNo IN
      (SELECT InvoiceNo
        FROM INVOICE_LINE
        WHERE PartNo IN
          (SELECT PartNo
            FROM PART
            WHERE NAME = 'flux capacitor') ;
```

The inner SELECT of the INVOICE table nests within the outer SELECT of the CUSTOMER table. The inner SELECT of the INVOICE_ LINE table nests within the outer SELECT of the INVOICE table. The inner SELECT of the PART table nests within the outer SELECT of the INVOICE_LINE table. The SELECT on the INVOICE table finds the CustomerID numbers of all customers who bought the flux capacitor product in the last 30 days. The outermost SELECT (on the CUSTOMER table) displays the first and last names of all customers whose CustomerID is retrieved by the inner SELECT statements.

LIKE and NOT LIKE

You can use the LIKE predicate to compare two character strings for a partial match. Partial matches are valuable if you don't know the exact form of the string for which you're searching. You can also use partial matches to retrieve multiple rows that contain similar strings in one of the table's columns.

To identify partial matches, SQL uses two wildcard characters. The percent sign (%) can stand for any string of characters that have zero or more characters. The underscore (_) stands for any single character. Table 5-2 provides some examples that show how to use LIKE.

TABLE 5-2 **SQL's LIKE Predicate**

Statement	Values Returned
WHERE String LIKE 'auto%'	auto
	automotive
	automobile
	automatic
	autocracy
WHERE String LIKE '%ode%'	code of conduct
	model citizen
WHERE String LIKE '_o_e'	mope
	tote
	rope
	love
	cone
	node

The NOT LIKE predicate retrieves all rows that don't satisfy a partial match, including one or more wildcard characters, as in the following example:

```
WHERE Email NOT LIKE '%@databasecentral.info'
```

This example returns all the rows in the table where the email address is not hosted at www.databasecentral.info.

TIP

You may want to search for a string that includes a percent sign or an underscore. In this case, you want SQL to interpret the percent sign as a percent sign and not as a wildcard character. You can conduct such a search by typing an escape character just prior to the character you want SQL to take literally. You can choose any character as the escape character, as long as that character doesn't appear in the string that you're testing, as shown in the following example:

```
SELECT Quote
    FROM BARTLETTS
    WHERE Quote LIKE '20#%'
        ESCAPE '#' ;
```

The % character is escaped by the preceding # sign, so the statement interprets this symbol as a percent sign rather than as a wildcard. You can escape an underscore or the escape character itself, in the same way. The preceding query, for example, would find the following quotation in *Bartlett's Familiar Quotations*:

```
20% of the salespeople produce 80% of the results.
```

The query would also find the following:

```
20%
```

NULL

The NULL predicate finds all rows where the value in the selected column is null. In the photographic paper price list table we describe in Chapter 4, several rows have null values in the Size11 column. You can retrieve their names by using a statement such as the following:

```
SELECT (PaperType)
    FROM PAPERS
    WHERE Size11Price IS NULL ;
```

This query returns the following values:

```
Dual-sided HW semigloss
Universal two-sided matte
Transparency
```

As you may expect, including the NOT keyword reverses the result, as in the following example:

```
SELECT (PaperType)
    FROM PAPERS
    WHERE Size11Price IS NOT NULL ;
```

This query returns all the rows in the table except the three that the preceding query returns.

WARNING

The statement Size11Price IS NULL is not the same as Size11Price = NULL. To illustrate this point, assume that, in the current row of the PAPERS table, both Size11Price and Size8Price are null. From this fact, you can draw the following conclusions:

>> Size11Price IS NULL is True.

>> Size8Price IS NULL is True.

>> (Size11Price IS NULL AND Size8Price IS NULL) is True.

>> Size11Price = Size8Price is unknown.

Size11Price = NULL is an illegal expression. Using the keyword NULL in a comparison is meaningless because the answer always returns as unknown.

Why is Size11Price = Size8Price defined as unknown, even though Size11Price and Size8Price have the same (null) value? Because NULL simply means, "I don't know." You don't know what Size11Price is, and you don't know what Size8Price is; therefore, you don't know whether those (unknown) values are the same. Maybe Size11Price is 9.95, and Size8Price is 8.95; or maybe Size11Price is 10.95, and Size8Price is 10.95. If you don't know both the Size11Price value and the Size8Price value, you can't say whether the two are the same.

ALL, SOME, and ANY

Thousands of years ago, the Greek philosopher Aristotle formulated a system of logic that became the basis for much of Western thought. The essence of this logic is to start with a set of premises that you know to be true, apply valid operations to these premises, and thereby arrive at new truths. The classic example of this procedure is as follows:

> *Premise 1:* All Greeks are human.
>
> *Premise 2:* All humans are mortal.
>
> *Conclusion:* All Greeks are mortal.

Another example:

> *Premise 1:* Some Greeks are women.
>
> *Premise 2:* All women are human.
>
> *Conclusion:* Some Greeks are human.

Another way of stating the same logical idea of this second example is as follows:

> If any Greeks are women and all women are human, then some Greeks are human.

The first example uses the universal quantifier ALL in both premises, enabling you to make a sound deduction about all Greeks in the conclusion. The second example uses the existential quantifier SOME in one premise, enabling you to make a deduction about some, but not all, Greeks in the conclusion. The third example uses the existential quantifier ANY, which is a synonym for SOME, to reach the same conclusion you reach in the second example.

Look at how SOME, ANY, and ALL apply in SQL.

Consider an example in baseball statistics. Baseball is a physically demanding sport, especially for pitchers. A pitcher must throw the baseball from the pitcher's mound, at speeds up to 100 miles per hour, to home plate between 90 and 150 times during a game. This effort can be very tiring, and many times, the starting pitcher becomes ineffective, and a relief pitcher must replace him before the game ends. Pitching an entire game is an outstanding achievement, regardless of whether the effort results in a victory.

Suppose you're keeping track of the number of complete games that all Major League Baseball pitchers pitch. In one table, you list all the American League pitchers, and in another table, you list all the National League pitchers. Both tables contain the players' first names, last names, and number of complete games pitched.

The American League permits a designated hitter (DH) (who isn't required to play a defensive position) to bat in place of any of the nine players who play defense. Usually, the DH bats for the pitcher because pitchers are notoriously poor hitters. (Pitchers must spend so much time and effort on perfecting their pitching that they don't have as much time to practice batting as the other players do.)

Say you speculate that, on average, American League starting pitchers throw more complete games than do National League starting pitchers. This is based on your observation that designated hitters enable hard-throwing, but weak-hitting, American League pitchers to stay in close games. Because the DH is already batting for them, the fact that they're poor hitters is not a liability. In the National League, however, a pinch hitter would replace a comparable National League pitcher in a close game because he would have a better chance at getting a hit. To test your idea, you formulate the following query:

```
SELECT FirstName, LastName
    FROM AMERICAN_LEAGUER
    WHERE CompleteGames > ALL
        (SELECT CompleteGames
            FROM NATIONAL_LEAGUER) ;
```

The subquery (the inner SELECT) returns a list, showing for every National League pitcher, the number of complete games he pitched. The outer query returns the first and last names of all American Leaguers who pitched more complete games than ALL of the National Leaguers. In other words, the query returns the names of those American League pitchers who pitched more complete games than the pitcher who has thrown the most complete games in the National League.

Consider the following similar statement:

```
SELECT FirstName, LastName
    FROM AMERICAN_LEAGUER
    WHERE CompleteGames > ANY
        (SELECT CompleteGames
            FROM NATIONAL_LEAGUER) ;
```

In this case, you use the existential quantifier ANY rather than the universal quantifier ALL. The subquery (the inner, nested query) is identical to the subquery in the previous example. This subquery retrieves a complete list of the complete game statistics for all the National League pitchers. The outer query returns the first and last names of all American League pitchers who pitched more complete games than ANY National League pitcher. Because you can be virtually certain that at least one National League pitcher hasn't pitched a complete game, the result probably includes all American League pitchers who've pitched at least one complete game.

If you replace the keyword ANY with the equivalent keyword SOME, the result is the same. If the statement that at least one National League pitcher hasn't pitched a complete game is a true statement, you can then say that SOME National League pitcher hasn't pitched a complete game.

EXISTS

You can use the EXISTS predicate in conjunction with a subquery to determine whether the subquery returns any rows. If the subquery returns at least one row, that result satisfies the EXISTS condition, and the outer query executes. Consider the following example:

```
SELECT FirstName, LastName
   FROM CUSTOMER
   WHERE EXISTS
     (SELECT DISTINCT CustomerID
        FROM INVOICE
        WHERE INVOICE.CustomerID =
           CUSTOMER.CustomerID);
```

The INVOICE table contains all your company's sales transactions. The table includes the CustomerID of the customer who makes each purchase, as well as other pertinent information. The CUSTOMER table contains each customer's first and last names, but no information about specific transactions.

The subquery in the preceding example returns a row for every customer who has made at least one purchase. The DISTINCT keyword assures you that you retrieve only one copy of each CustomerID, even if a customer has made more than one purchase. The outer query returns the first and last names of the customers who made the purchases that the INVOICE table records.

UNIQUE

As you do with the EXISTS predicate, you use the UNIQUE predicate with a subquery. Although the EXISTS predicate evaluates to TRUE only if the subquery returns at least one row, the UNIQUE predicate evaluates to TRUE only if no two rows that the subquery returns are identical. In other words, the UNIQUE predicate evaluates to TRUE *only* if all rows that its subquery returns are unique. Consider the following example:

```
SELECT FirstName, LastName
    FROM CUSTOMER
    WHERE UNIQUE
        (SELECT CustomerID FROM INVOICE
            WHERE INVOICE.CustomerID =
                CUSTOMER.CustomerID);
```

This statement retrieves the names of all first-time customers for whom the INVOICE table records only one sale. Two null values are considered to be not equal to each other and, thus, unique. When the UNIQUE keyword is applied to a result table that contains only two null rows, the UNIQUE predicate evaluates to True.

DISTINCT

The DISTINCT predicate is similar to the UNIQUE predicate, except in the way it treats nulls. If all the values in a result table are UNIQUE, they're also DISTINCT from each other. However, unlike the result for the UNIQUE predicate, if the DISTINCT keyword is applied to a result table that contains only two null rows, the DISTINCT predicate evaluates to False. By default, two null values are *not* considered distinct from each other, while at the same time they are considered to be unique. This strange situation seems contradictory, but there's a reason for it. In some situations, you may want to treat two null values as different from each other, whereas in other situations, you want to treat them as if they're the same. In the first case, use the UNIQUE predicate. In the second case, use the DISTINCT predicate. However, you can combine the UNIQUE and DISTINCT predicates to treat null values as also being distinct. The UNIQUE NULLS NOT DISTINCT predicate combination considers two null values as being distinct, as well as unique.

OVERLAPS

You use the OVERLAPS predicate to determine whether two time intervals overlap each other. This predicate is useful for avoiding scheduling conflicts. If the two intervals overlap, the predicate returns a True value. If they don't overlap, the predicate returns a False value.

You can specify an interval in two ways: either as a start time and an end time or as a start time and a duration. Following are a few examples:

```
(TIME '2:55:00', INTERVAL '1' HOUR)
OVERLAPS
(TIME '3:30:00', INTERVAL '2' HOUR)
```

The preceding example returns a True because 3:30 is less than one hour after 2:55.

```
(TIME '9:00:00', TIME '9:30:00')
OVERLAPS
(TIME '9:29:00', TIME '9:31:00')
```

The preceding example returns a True because you have a one-minute overlap between the two intervals.

```
(TIME '9:00:00', TIME '10:00:00')
OVERLAPS
(TIME '10:15:00', INTERVAL '3' HOUR)
```

The preceding example returns a False because the two intervals don't overlap.

```
(TIME '9:00:00', TIME '9:30:00')
OVERLAPS
(TIME '9:30:00', TIME '9:35:00')
```

This example returns a False because even though the two intervals are contiguous, they don't overlap.

MATCH

Maintaining consistency in the data fields stored in a multitable database (called *referential integrity*) is important. You can lose integrity by adding a row to a child table that doesn't have a corresponding row in the child's parent table. You can cause similar problems by deleting a row from a parent table if rows corresponding to that row exist in a child table.

Say that your business has a CUSTOMER table that keeps track of all your customers and a TRANSACT table that records all sales transactions. You don't want to add a row to TRANSACT until after you enter the customer making the purchase into the CUSTOMER table. You also don't want to delete a customer from the CUSTOMER table if that customer made purchases that exist in the TRANSACT table. Before you perform an insertion or deletion, you may want to check the candidate row to make sure that inserting or deleting that row doesn't cause integrity problems. The MATCH predicate can perform such a check.

To examine the MATCH predicate, we use an example that employs the CUSTOMER and TRANSACT tables. CustomerID is the primary key of the CUSTOMER table and acts as a foreign key in the TRANSACT table. Every row in the CUSTOMER table must have a unique, nonnull CustomerID. CustomerID isn't unique in the TRANSACT table because repeat customers buy more than once. This situation is fine and does not threaten integrity because CustomerID is a foreign key rather than a primary key in that table.

TIP

Seemingly, CustomerID can be null in the TRANSACT table because someone can walk in off the street, buy something, and walk out before you get a chance to enter their name and address into the CUSTOMER table. This situation can create a row in the child table with no corresponding row in the parent table. To overcome this problem, you can create a generic customer in the CUSTOMER table and assign all such anonymous sales to that customer.

Say that a customer steps up to the cash register and claims that they bought a flux capacitor on January 15, 2019. They now want to return the device because they've discovered that their DeLorean lacks time circuits, so the flux capacitor is of no use. You can verify their claim by searching your TRANSACT database for a match. First, you must retrieve their CustomerID into the variable vcustid; then you can use the following syntax:

```
... WHERE (:vcustid, 'flux capacitor',
        '2019-01-15')
           MATCH
           (SELECT CustomerID, ProductName, Date
               FROM TRANSACT)
```

If a sale exists for that customer ID for that product on that date, the MATCH predicate returns a True value. Take back the product and refund the customer's money. (*Note:* If any values in the first argument of the MATCH predicate are null, a True value always returns.)

The general form of the MATCH predicate is as follows:

```
Row_value MATCH  [UNIQUE] [SIMPLE| PARTIAL | FULL
    ] Subquery
```

The UNIQUE, SIMPLE, PARTIAL, and FULL options relate to rules that come into play if the row value expression R has one or more columns that are null. The rules for the MATCH predicate are a copy of corresponding referential integrity rules.

The MATCH predicate and referential integrity

Referential integrity rules require that the values of a column or columns in one table match the values of a column or columns in another table. You refer to the columns in the first table as the *foreign key* and the columns in the second table as the *primary key* or *unique key*. For example, you may declare the column EmpDeptNo in an EMPLOYEE table as a foreign key that references the DeptNo column of a DEPT table. This matchup ensures that if you record an employee in the EMPLOYEE table as working in department 123, a row appears in the DEPT table, where DeptNo is 123.

This situation is fairly straightforward if the foreign key and primary key both consist of a single column. The two keys can, however, consist of multiple columns. The DeptNo value, for example, may be unique only within a Location; therefore, to uniquely identify a DEPT row, you must specify both a Location and a DeptNo. If both the Boston and Tampa offices have a department 123, you need to identify the departments as ('Boston' , '123') and ('Tampa' , '123'). In this case, the EMPLOYEE table needs two columns to identify a DEPT. Call those columns EmpLoc and EmpDeptNo. If an employee works in department 123 in Boston, the EmpLoc and EmpDeptNo values are 'Boston' and '123'. And the foreign key declaration in EMPLOYEE is as follows:

```
FOREIGN KEY (EmpLoc, EmpDeptNo)
    REFERENCES DEPT (Location, DeptNo)
```

Drawing valid conclusions from your data is complicated immensely if the data contains nulls. Sometimes you want to treat null-containing data one way, and sometimes you want to treat it another way. The UNIQUE, SIMPLE, PARTIAL, and FULL keywords specify different ways of treating data that contains nulls. If your data does not contain any null values, you can save yourself a lot of head-scratching by merely skipping to the section called "Logical connectives" later in this chapter. If your data *does* contain null values, drop out of Evelyn Wood speed-reading mode now and read the following paragraphs slowly and carefully. Each paragraph presents a different situation with respect to null values and tells how the MATCH predicate handles it.

If the values of EmpLoc and EmpDeptNo are both nonnull or both null, the referential integrity rules are the same as for single-column keys with values that are null or nonnull. But if EmpLoc is null and EmpDeptNo is nonnull — or EmpLoc is nonnull and EmpDeptNo is null — you need new rules. What should the rules be if you insert or update the EMPLOYEE table with EmpLoc and EmpDeptNo values of (NULL, '123') or ('Boston', NULL)? You have six main alternatives: SIMPLE, PARTIAL, and FULL, each either with or without the UNIQUE keyword. The UNIQUE keyword, if present, means that a matching row in the subquery result table must be unique in order for the predicate to evaluate to a True value. If both components of the row value expression R are null, the MATCH predicate returns a True value regardless of the contents of the subquery result table being compared.

If neither component of the row value expression R is null, SIMPLE is specified, UNIQUE is not specified, and at least one row in the subquery result table matches R, the MATCH predicate returns a True value. Otherwise, it returns a False value.

If neither component of the row value expression R is null, SIMPLE is specified, UNIQUE is specified, and at least one row in the subquery result table is both unique and matches R, the MATCH predicate returns a True value. Otherwise, it returns a False value.

If any component of the row value expression R is null and SIMPLE is specified, the MATCH predicate returns a True value.

If any component of the row value expression R is nonnull, PARTIAL is specified, UNIQUE is not specified, and the nonnull parts of at least one row in the subquery result table matches R, the MATCH predicate returns a True value. Otherwise, it returns a False value.

If any component of the row value expression R is nonnull, PARTIAL is specified, UNIQUE is specified, and the nonnull parts of R match the nonnull parts of at least one unique row in the subquery result table, the MATCH predicate returns a True value. Otherwise, it returns a False value.

If neither component of the row value expression R is null, FULL is specified, UNIQUE is not specified, and at least one row in the subquery result table matches R, the MATCH predicate returns a True value. Otherwise, it returns a False value.

If neither component of the row value expression R is null, FULL is specified, UNIQUE is specified, and at least one row in the subquery result table is both unique and matches R, the MATCH predicate returns a True value. Otherwise, it returns a False value.

If any component of the row value expression R is null and FULL is specified, the MATCH predicate returns a False value.

Logical connectives

Often, as a number of previous examples show, applying one condition in a query isn't enough to return the rows that you want from a table. In some cases, the rows must satisfy two or more conditions. In other cases, if a row satisfies any of two or more conditions, it qualifies for retrieval. On other occasions, you want to retrieve only rows that don't satisfy a specified condition. To meet these needs, SQL offers the logical connectives AND, OR, and NOT.

AND

If multiple conditions must all be `True` before you can retrieve a row, use the `AND` logical connective. Consider the following example:

```
SELECT InvoiceNo, SaleDate, SalesPerson, TotalSale
    FROM SALES
    WHERE SaleDate >= '2019-01-16'
        AND SaleDate <= '2019-01-22' ;
```

The `WHERE` clause must meet the following two conditions:

>> SaleDate must be greater than or equal to January 16, 2019.

>> SaleDate must be less than or equal to January 22, 2019.

Only rows that record sales occurring during the week of January 16 meet both conditions. The query returns only these rows.

WARNING

Notice that the `AND` connective is strictly logical. This restriction can sometimes be confusing because people commonly use the word *and* with a looser meaning. Suppose, for example, that your boss says to you, "I'd like to see the sales for Acheson and Bryant." She said, "Acheson and Bryant," so you may write the following SQL query:

```
SELECT *
    FROM SALES
    WHERE Salesperson = 'Acheson'
        AND Salesperson = 'Bryant';
```

Well, don't take that answer back to your boss. The following query is more like what they had in mind:

```
SELECT *
    FROM SALES
    WHERE Salesperson IN ('Acheson', 'Bryant') ;
```

The first query won't return anything, because none of the sales in the SALES table were made by *both* Acheson and Bryant. The second query returns the information on all sales made by either Acheson or Bryant, which is probably what the boss wanted.

OR

If any one of two or more conditions must be True to qualify a row for retrieval, use the OR logical connective, as in the following example:

```
SELECT InvoiceNo, SaleDate, Salesperson, TotalSale
    FROM SALES
        WHERE Salesperson = 'Bryant'
            OR TotalSale > 200 ;
```

This query retrieves all of Bryant's sales, regardless of how large, as well as all sales of more than $200, regardless of who made the sales.

NOT

The NOT connective negates a condition. If the condition normally returns a True value, adding NOT causes the same condition to return a False value. If a condition normally returns a False value, adding NOT causes the condition to return a True value. Consider the following example:

```
SELECT InvoiceNo, SaleDate, Salesperson, TotalSale
    FROM SALES
        WHERE NOT (Salesperson = 'Bryant') ;
```

This query returns rows for all sales transactions completed by salespeople other than Bryant.

WARNING

When you use AND, OR, or NOT, sometimes the scope of the connective isn't clear. To be safe, use parentheses to make sure that SQL applies the connective to the predicate you want. In the preceding example, the NOT connective applies to the entire predicate (Salesperson = 'Bryant').

GROUP BY clauses

Sometimes, instead of retrieving individual records, you want to know something about a group of records. The GROUP BY clause is the tool you need. We use the AdventureWorks2022 sample database designed to work with Microsoft SQL Server 2022 for the following examples.

SQL Server Express is a version of Microsoft SQL Server that you can download for free from www.microsoft.com.

Suppose you're the sales manager, and you want to look at the performance of your sales force. You could do a simple SELECT such as the following:

```
SELECT SalesOrderId, OrderDate, LastName, TotalDue
    FROM Sales.SalesOrderHeader, Person.Person
    WHERE BusinessEntityID = SalesPersonID
        AND OrderDate >= '2011-07-01'
        AND OrderDate <= '2011-07-31'
```

You would receive a result similar to that shown in Figure 5-1. In this database, SalesOrderHeader is a table in the Sales schema and Person is a table in the Person schema. BusinessEntityID is the primary key of the SalesOrderHeader table, and SalesPersonID is the primary key of the Person table. SalesOrderID, OrderDate, and TotalDue are rows in the SalesOrderHeader table, and LastName is a row in the Person table.

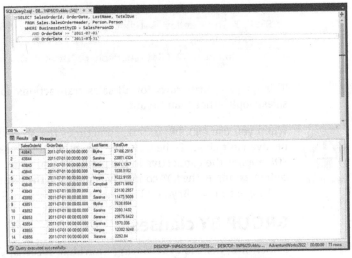

FIGURE 5-1: The result set for retrieval of sales for July 2011.

This result gives you some idea of how well your salespeople are doing because relatively few sales are involved. Seventy-five rows were returned. However, in real life, a company would have many more sales, and it wouldn't be as easy to tell whether sales objectives were being met. To do that, you can combine the GROUP BY clause with one of the *aggregate functions* (also called *set functions*) to get a quantitative picture of sales performance. For example, you can see which salesperson is selling more of the profitable high-ticket items by using the average (AVG) function as follows:

```
SELECT LastName, AVG(TotalDue)
    FROM Sales.SalesOrderHeader, Person.Person
    WHERE BusinessEntityID = SalesPersonID
        AND OrderDate >= '2011-07-01'
        AND OrderDate <= '2011-07-31'
    GROUP BY LastName;
```

You would receive a result similar to that shown in Figure 5-2. The GROUP BY clause causes records to be grouped by LastName and the groups to be sorted in ascending alphabetical order.

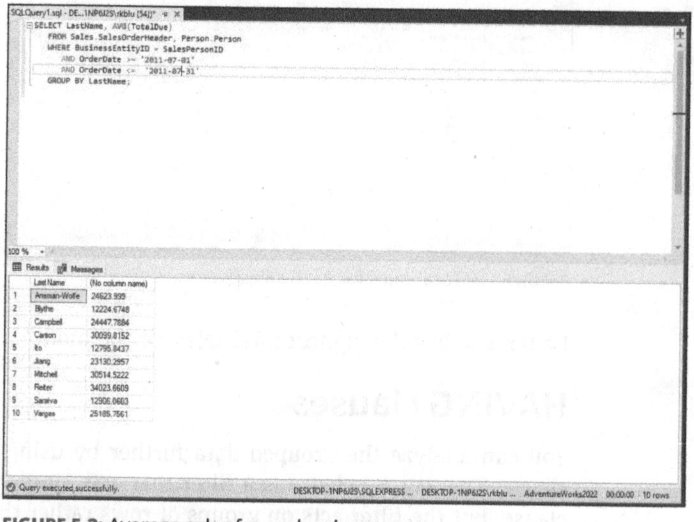

FIGURE 5-2: Average sales for each salesperson.

As shown in Figure 5-2, Reiter has the highest average sales. You can compare total sales with a similar query — this time using SUM:

```
SELECT LastName, SUM(TotalDue)
    FROM Sales.SalesOrderHeader, Person.Person
```

```
WHERE BusinessEntityID = SalesPersonID
    AND OrderDate >= '2011-07-01'
    AND OrderDate <= '2011-07-31'
GROUP BY LastName;
```

This gives the result shown in Figure 5-3. As in the previous example, the GROUP BY clause causes records to be grouped by LastName and the groups to be sorted in ascending alphabetical order.

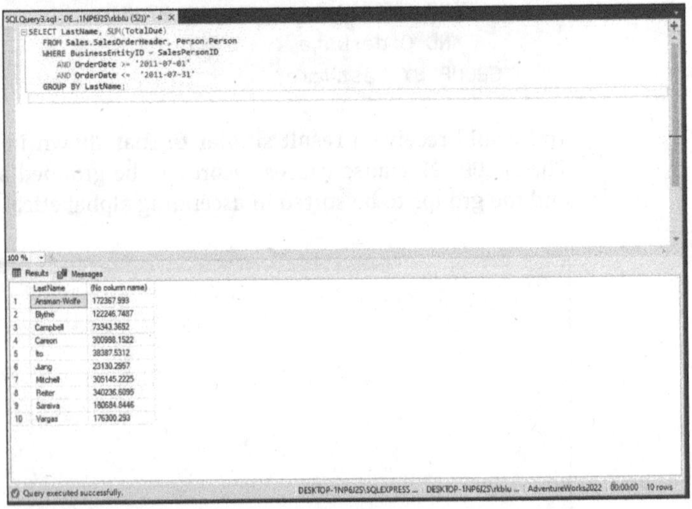

FIGURE 5-3: Total sales for each salesperson.

Reiter also has the highest total sales for the month.

HAVING clauses

You can analyze the grouped data further by using the HAVING clause. The HAVING clause is a filter that acts similar to a WHERE clause, but the filter acts on groups of rows rather than on individual rows. To illustrate the function of the HAVING clause, suppose Saraiva has just resigned, and the sales manager wants to display the overall data for the other salespeople. You can exclude Saraiva's sales from the grouped data by using a HAVING clause as follows:

```
SELECT LastName, SUM(TotalDue)
    FROM Sales.SalesOrderHeader, Person.Person
```

```
WHERE BusinessEntityID = SalesPersonID
    AND OrderDate >= '2011-07-01'
    AND OrderDate <= '2011-07-31'
GROUP BY LastName
HAVING LastName <> 'Saraiva';
```

This gives the result shown in Figure 5-4. Only rows where the salesperson is *not* Saraiva are returned. As before, the GROUP BY clause causes records to be grouped by LastName and the groups to be sorted in ascending alphabetical order.

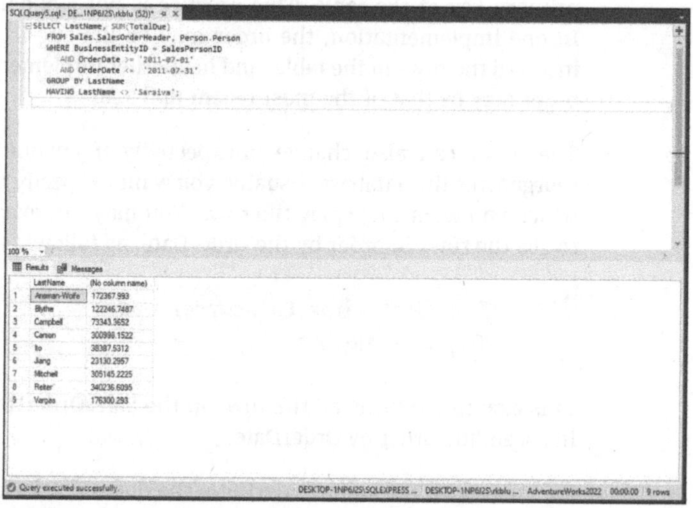

FIGURE 5-4: Total sales for all salespeople except Saraiva.

ORDER BY clauses

You can use the ORDER BY clause to display the output table of a query in either ascending or descending alphabetical order. Whereas the GROUP BY clause gathers rows into groups and sorts the groups into alphabetical order, ORDER BY sorts individual rows. The ORDER BY clause must be the last clause that you specify in a query. If the query also contains a GROUP BY clause, the clause first arranges the output rows into groups. The ORDER BY clause then sorts the rows within each group. If you have no GROUP BY clause, the statement considers the entire table as a group, and the ORDER BY clause sorts all its rows according to the column(s) that the ORDER BY clause specifies.

To illustrate this point, consider the data in the SalesOrderHeader table. The SalesOrderHeader table contains columns for SalesOrderID, OrderDate, DueDate, ShipDate, and SalesPersonID, among other things. If you use the following example, you see all the SALES data:

```
SELECT * FROM Sales.SalesOrderHeader ;
```

Theoretically, the order in which the records are listed is arbitrary. If you're using the Microsoft SQL Server Management Studio, it orders the result records by SalesOrderID, because that's the primary key of the table. This practice is not standard, though. In one implementation, the order may be the one in which you inserted the rows in the table, and in another implementation, the order may be that of the most recent updates.

The order can also change unexpectedly if anyone physically reorganizes the database. Usually, you want to specify the order in which you want to display the rows. You may, for example, want to see the rows in order by the OrderDate, as follows:

```
SELECT * FROM Sales.SalesOrderHeader
    ORDER BY OrderDate ;
```

This example returns all the rows in the SalesOrderHeader table, in ascending order by OrderDate.

For rows with the same OrderDate, the default order depends on the implementation. You can, however, specify how to sort the rows that share the same OrderDate. You may want to see the orders for each OrderDate in order by SalesOrderID, as follows:

```
SELECT * FROM Sales.SalesOrderHeader
    ORDER BY OrderDate, SalesOrderID ;
```

This example first orders the sales by OrderDate; then for each OrderDate, it orders the sales by SalesOrderID. But don't confuse that example with the following query:

```
SELECT * FROM Sales.SalesOrderHeader
    ORDER BY SalesOrderID, OrderDate ;
```

This query first orders the sales by SalesOrderID. Then for each different SalesOrderID, the query orders the sales by OrderDate. This probably won't yield the result you want because it's unlikely that multiple order dates exist for a single sales order number.

The following query is another example of how SQL can return data:

```
SELECT * FROM Sales.SalesOrderHeader
    ORDER BY SalesPersonID, OrderDate ;
```

This example first orders by salesperson and then by order date. After you look at the data in that order, you may want to invert it, as follows:

```
SELECT * FROM Sales.SalesPersonID
    ORDER BY OrderDate, SalesPersonID ;
```

This example orders the rows first by order date and then by salesperson.

All these ordering examples are ascending (ASC), which is the default sort order. In the AdventureWorks2022 sample database, this last SELECT would show earlier sales first and, within a given date, would show sales for 'Ansman-Wolfe' before 'Blythe'. If you prefer descending (DESC) order, you can specify this order for one or more of the order columns, as follows:

```
SELECT * FROM Sales.SalesPersonID
    ORDER BY OrderDate DESC, SalesPersonID ASC;
```

This example specifies a descending order for order date, showing the more recent orders first, and an ascending order for salespeople.

TIP

SQL:2023 has cleared up one bit of confusion with how the ORDER BY clause works. Prior to SQL:2023, the standard specified that a SELECT query was not allowed to use a data field in the ORDER BY clause that wasn't included as part of the SELECT data fields. However, almost all SQL implementations ignored that rule and allowed you to order the result set by a data field not included in the result set. SQL:2023 has incorporated that behavior as part of the standard, so if you order the result set using a data field that isn't contained in the result set, you're staying within the SQL:2023 standard.

Chapter **6**

Querying Multiple Tables with Subqueries

R elational databases have multiple tables. That's where the word *relational* comes from — multiple tables that relate to each other in some way. One consequence of the distribution of data across multiple tables is that most queries need to pull data from more than one of them. There are a couple of ways to do this. One is to use relational operators, which we cover in the next chapter. The other method is to use subqueries, which is the subject of this chapter.

Introducing Subqueries

A *subquery* is an SQL statement embedded within another SQL statement. It's possible for a subquery to be embedded within another subquery, which is in turn embedded within an outermost SQL statement. Theoretically, there is no limit to the number of levels of subquery that an SQL statement may include, although any given implementation has a practical limit. A key feature of a subquery is that the table(s) that it references need not be the same as the table(s) referenced by its enclosing query. This has the effect of returning results based on the information in multiple tables.

Subqueries are located within the WHERE clause of their enclosing statement. Their function is to set the search conditions for the WHERE clause. The combination of a subquery and its enclosing query is called a *nested query*. Different kinds of nested queries produce different results. Some subqueries produce a list of values that is then used as input by the enclosing statement. Other subqueries produce a single value that the enclosing statement then evaluates with a comparison operator. A third kind of subquery, called a *correlated subquery*, operates differently, and we discuss it in the upcoming "Correlated subqueries" section.

Subqueries that return multiple values

A key concern of many businesses is inventory control. When you're building products that are made up of various parts, you want to make sure that you have an adequate supply of all the parts. If just one part is in short supply, it could bring the entire manufacturing operation to a screeching halt. To see how many products are impacted by the lack of a part they need, you can use a subquery.

Subqueries that retrieve rows satisfying a condition

Suppose your company (Penguin Electronics, Inc.) manufactures a variety of electronic products, such as audio amplifiers, FM radio tuners, and handheld metal detectors. You keep track of inventory of all your products — as well as all the parts that go into their manufacture — in a relational database. The database has a PRODUCTS table that holds the inventory levels of finished products and a PARTS table that holds the inventory levels of the parts that go into the products.

A part could be included in multiple products, and each product is made up of multiple parts. This means that there is a many-to-many relationship between the PRODUCTS table and the PARTS table, which for a relational database can make things somewhat complicated. You'll need to insert an intersection table between PRODUCTS and PARTS, transforming the problematical many-to-many relationship into two easier-to-deal-with one-to-many relationships. The intersection table, named PROD_PARTS, takes the primary keys of PRODUCTS and PARTS as its only attributes.

You can create these three tables with the following code:

```
CREATE TABLE PRODUCTS (
    ProductID              INTEGER        PRIMARY KEY,
    ProductName            CHAR (30),
    ProductDescription     CHAR (50),
    ListPrice              NUMERIC (9,2),
    QuantityInStock        INTEGER) ;

CREATE TABLE PARTS (
    PartID                 INTEGER        PRIMARY KEY,
    PartName               CHAR (30),
    PartDescription        CHAR (50),
    QuantityInStock        INTEGER) ;

CREATE TABLE PROD_PARTS (
    ProductID              INTEGER        NOT NULL,
    PartID                 INTEGER        NOT NULL) ;
```

Suppose some of your products include an APM-17 DC analog panel meter. Now you find, to your horror, that you're completely out of the APM-17 part. You can't complete the manufacture of any product that includes it. It's time for management to take some emergency actions. One is to check on the status of any outstanding orders to the supplier of the APM-17 panel meters. Another is to notify the sales department to stop selling all products that include the APM-17 and switch to promoting products that don't include it.

To discover which products include the APM-17, you can use a nested query such as the following:

```
SELECT ProductID
    FROM PROD_PARTS
    WHERE PartID IN
        (SELECT PartID
            FROM PARTS
            WHERE PartDescription = 'APM-17') ;
```

SQL processes the innermost query first, so it queries the PARTS table, returning the PartID of every row in the PARTS table where the PartDescription is APM-17. There should be only one such row. Only one part should have a description of APM-17. The outer query uses the IN keyword to find all the rows in the

PROD_PARTS table that include the PartID that appears in the result set from the inner query. The outer query then extracts from the PROD_PARTS table the ProductIDs of all the products that include the APM-17 part. These are the products that the Sales department should stop selling.

Subqueries that retrieve rows that don't satisfy a condition

Because sales are the lifeblood of any business, it's even more important to determine which products the Sales team can continue to sell than it is to tell them what not to sell. You can do this with another nested query. Use the query just executed in the preceding section as a base, add one more layer of query to it, and return the ProductIDs of all the products not affected by the APM-17 shortage:

```
SELECT ProductID
    FROM PROD_PARTS
    WHERE ProductID NOT IN
        (SELECT ProductID
            FROM PROD_PARTS
            WHERE PartID IN
                (SELECT PartID
                    FROM PARTS
                    WHERE PartDescription = 'APM-17') ;
```

The two inner queries return the ProductIDs of all the products that include the APM-17 part. The outer query returns all the ProductIDs of all the products that are not included in the result set from the inner queries. This final result set is the list of ProductIDs of products that do not include the APM-17 analog panel meter.

Subqueries that return a single value

Introducing a subquery with one of the six comparison operators (=, <>, <, <=, >, >=) is often useful. In such a case, the expression preceding the operator evaluates to a single value, and the subquery following the operator must also evaluate to a single value. An exception is the case of the *quantified comparison operator*, which is a comparison operator followed by a quantifier (ANY, SOME, or ALL).

To illustrate a case in which a subquery returns a single value, look at another piece of the Penguin Electronics database. It contains a CUSTOMER table that holds information about the companies that buy Penguin products. It also contains a CONTACT table that holds personal data about individuals at each of Penguin's customer organizations. The following code creates Penguin's CUSTOMER and CONTACT tables:

```
CREATE TABLE CUSTOMER (
    CustomerID          INTEGER         PRIMARY KEY,
    Company             CHAR (40),
    Address1            CHAR (50),
    Address2            CHAR (50),
    City                CHAR (25),
    State               CHAR (2),
    PostalCode          CHAR (10),
    Phone               CHAR (13)) ;
CREATE TABLE CONTACT (
    CustomerID          INTEGER         PRIMARY KEY,
    FirstName           CHAR (15),
    LastName            CHAR (20),
    Phone               CHAR (13),
    Email               CHAR (30),
    Fax                 CHAR (13),
    Notes               CHAR (100),
    CONSTRAINT ContactFK FOREIGN KEY (CustomerID)
      REFERENCES CUSTOMER (CustomerID)) ;
```

Say that you want to look at the contact information for the customer named Baker Electronic Sales, but you don't remember that company's CustomerID. Use a nested query like this one to recover the information you want:

```
SELECT *
  FROM CONTACT
      WHERE CustomerID =
          (SELECT CustomerID
             FROM CUSTOMER
                 WHERE Company =
                     'Baker Electronic Sales') ;
```

The result looks something like this:

CustomerID	FirstName	LastName	Phone	Notes
787	David	Lee	555-876-3456	Likes to visit El Pollo Loco when in Cali.

You can now call Dave at Baker and tell him about this month's special sale on metal detectors.

When you use a subquery in an "=" comparison, the subquery's SELECT list must specify a single column (CustomerID in the example). When the subquery is executed, it must return a single row in order to have a single value for the comparison.

In this example, we assume that the CUSTOMER table has only one row with a Company value of Baker Electronic Sales. If the CREATE TABLE statement for CUSTOMER specified a UNIQUE constraint for Company, such a statement guarantees that the subquery in the preceding example returns a single value (or no value). Subqueries like the one in the example, however, are commonly used on columns not specified to be UNIQUE. In such cases, you're relying on some other reasons for believing that the column has no duplicates.

If more than one CUSTOMER has a value of Baker Electronic Sales in the Company column (perhaps in different states), the subquery raises an error.

If no Customer with such a company name exists, the subquery is treated as if it were null, and the comparison becomes unknown. In this case, the WHERE clause returns no row (because it returns only rows with the condition True and filters rows with the condition False or Unknown). This would probably happen, for example, if someone misspelled the COMPANY as Baker Electronics Sales.

Although the equals operator (=) is the most common, you can use any of the other five comparison operators in a similar structure. For every row in the table specified in the enclosing statement's FROM clause, the single value returned by the subquery is compared to the expression in the enclosing statement's WHERE clause. If the comparison gives a True value, a row is added to the result table.

You can guarantee that a subquery returns a single value if you include a set function in it. Set functions, also known as *aggregate functions*, always return a single value. (We describe set functions in Chapter 4.) Of course, this way of returning a single value is helpful only if you want the result of a set function.

Say you're a Penguin Electronics salesperson, and you need to earn a big commission check to pay for some unexpected bills. You decide to concentrate on selling Penguin's most expensive product. You can find out what that product is with a nested query:

```
SELECT ProductID, ProductName, ListPrice
    FROM PRODUCT
        WHERE ListPrice =
            (SELECT MAX(ListPrice)
                FROM PRODUCT) ;
```

This is an example of a nested query where both the subquery and the enclosing statement operate on the same table. The subquery returns a single value: the maximum list price in the PRODUCTS table. The outer query retrieves all rows from the PRODUCTS table that have that list price.

The next example shows a comparison subquery that uses a comparison operator other than =:

```
SELECT ProductID, ProductName, ListPrice
    FROM PRODUCTS
        WHERE ListPrice <
            (SELECT AVG(ListPrice)
                FROM PRODUCTS) ;
```

The subquery returns a single value: the average list price in the PRODUCTS table. The outer query retrieves all rows from the PRODUCTS table that have a list price less than the average list price.

In the original SQL standard, a comparison could have only one subquery, and it had to be on the right side of the comparison. SQL:1999 allowed either or both operands of the comparison to be subqueries, and later versions of SQL retain that expanded capability.

Quantified subqueries: Returning a single value

One way to make sure a subquery returns a single value is to introduce it with a quantified comparison operator. The universal quantifier ALL, and the existential quantifiers SOME and ANY, when combined with a comparison operator, process the result set returned by the inner subquery, reducing it to a single value.

Consider an example. From the 1960s through the 1980s, there was fierce competition between Ford and Chevrolet to produce the most powerful cars. Both companies had small-block V8 engines that went into Mustangs, Camaros, and other performance-oriented vehicles.

Power is measured in units of horsepower. In general, a larger engine delivers more horsepower, all other things being equal. Because the displacements (sizes) of the engines varied from one model to another, it's unfair to look only at horsepower. A better measure of the efficiency of an engine is horsepower per displacement. Displacement is measured in cubic inches (CID). Table 6-1 shows the year, displacement, and horsepower ratings for Ford small-block V8s between 1960 and 1980.

TABLE 6-1 Ford Small-Block V8s, 1960–1980

Year	Displacement (CID)	Maximum Horsepower	Notes
1962	221	145	
1963	289	225	4bbl carburetor
1965	289	271	289HP model
1965	289	306	Shelby GT350
1969	351	290	4bbl carburetor
1975	302	140	Emission regulations

The Shelby GT350 was a classic muscle car — not a typical car for the weekday commute. Emission regulations taking effect in the early 1970s halved power output and brought an end to the muscle car era. Table 6-2 shows what Chevy put out during the same time frame.

TABLE 6-2 Chevy Small-Block V8s, 1960–1980

Year	Displacement (CID)	Maximum Horsepower	Notes
1960	283	315	
1962	327	375	
1967	350	295	
1968	302	290	
1968	307	200	
1969	350	370	Corvette
1970	400	265	
1975	262	110	Emission regulations

Here, again, you see the effect of the emission regulations that kicked in circa 1971 — a drastic drop in horsepower per displacement.

Use the following code to create tables to hold these data items:

```
CREATE TABLE Ford (
    EngineID            INTEGER        PRIMARY KEY,
    ModelYear           CHAR (4),
    Displacement        NUMERIC (5,2),
    MaxHP               NUMERIC (5,2),
    Notes               CHAR (30)) ;

CREATE TABLE Chevy (
    EngineID            INTEGER        PRIMARY KEY,
    ModelYear           CHAR (4),
    Displacement        NUMERIC (5,2),
    MaxHP               NUMERIC (5,2),
    Notes               CHAR (30)) ;
```

After filling these tables with the data in Tables 6-1 and 6-2, you can run some queries. Suppose you're a dyed-in-the-wool Chevy fan and you're quite certain that the most powerful Chevrolet has a higher horsepower-to-displacement ratio than any of the Fords. To verify that assumption, enter the following query:

```
SELECT *
    FROM Chevy
    WHERE (MaxHP/Displacement) > ALL
        (SELECT (MaxHP/Displacement) FROM Ford) ;
```

This returns the result shown in Figure 6-1.

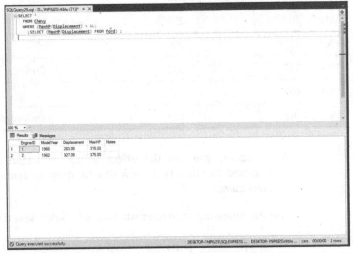

FIGURE 6-1: Chevy muscle cars with horsepower to displacement ratios higher than any of the Fords listed.

The subquery — SELECT (MaxHP/Displacement) FROM Ford — returns the horsepower-to-displacement ratios of all the Ford engines in the Ford table. The ALL quantifier says to return only those records from the Chevy table that have horsepower-to-displacement ratios higher than all the ratios returned for the Ford engines. Two different Chevy engines had higher ratios than any Ford engine of that era, including the highly regarded Shelby GT350. Ford fans should not be bothered by this result, however. There's more to what makes a car awesome than just the horsepower-to-displacement ratio.

What if you had made the opposite assumption? What if you had entered the following query?

```
SELECT *
    FROM Ford
    WHERE (MaxHP/Displacement) > ALL
        (SELECT (MaxHP/Displacement) FROM Chevy) ;
```

Because none of the Ford engines has a higher horsepower-to-displacement ratio than *all* of the Chevy engines, the query doesn't return any rows.

Correlated subqueries

In all the nested queries we show in the previous sections, the inner subquery is executed first, and then its result is applied to the outer enclosing statement. A *correlated subquery* first finds the table and row specified by the enclosing statement, and then executes the subquery on the row in the subquery's table that correlates with the current row of the enclosing statement's table.

Using a subquery as an existence test

Subqueries introduced with the EXISTS or the NOT EXISTS keyword are examples of correlated subqueries. The subquery either returns one or more rows, or it returns none. If it returns at least one row, the EXISTS predicate succeeds and the enclosing statement performs its action. In the same circumstances, the NOT EXISTS predicate fails and the enclosing statement does not perform its action. After one row of the enclosing statement's table is processed, the same operation is performed on the next row. This action is repeated until every row in the enclosing statement's table has been processed.

TESTING FOR EXISTENCE

Say that you're a salesperson for Penguin Electronics and you want to call your primary contact people at all of Penguin's customer organizations in New Hampshire. Try the following query:

```
SELECT *
    FROM CONTACT
    WHERE EXISTS
        (SELECT *
```

```
        FROM CUSTOMER
        WHERE State = 'NH'
            AND CONTACT.CustomerID =
                CUSTOMER.CustomerID) ;
```

Notice the reference to CONTACT.CustomerID, which is referencing a column from the outer query and comparing it with another column, CUSTOMER.CustomerID, from the inner query. For each candidate row of the outer query, you evaluate the inner query, using the CustomerID value from the current CONTACT row of the outer query in the WHERE clause of the inner query.

The CustomerID column links the CONTACT table to the CUSTOMER table. SQL looks at the first record in the CONTACT table, finds the row in the CUSTOMER table that has the same CustomerID, and checks that row's State field. If CUSTOMER.State = 'NH', the current CONTACT row is added to the result table. The next CONTACT record is then processed in the same way, and so on, until the entire CONTACT table has been processed. Because the query specifies SELECT * FROM CONTACT, all the CONTACT table's fields are returned, including the contact's name and phone number.

TESTING FOR NONEXISTENCE

In the previous example, the Penguin salesperson wants to know the names and numbers of the contact people of all the customers in New Hampshire. Imagine that a second salesperson is responsible for all of the United States except New Hampshire. They can retrieve their contacts by using NOT EXISTS in a query similar to the preceding one:

```
SELECT *
    FROM CONTACT
    WHERE NOT EXISTS
        (SELECT *
            FROM CUSTOMER
            WHERE State = 'NH'
                AND CONTACT.CustomerID =
                    CUSTOMER.CustomerID) ;
```

Every row in CONTACT for which the subquery does not return a row is added to the result table.

Introducing a correlated subquery with the IN keyword

As we note earlier in this chapter, subqueries introduced by IN or by a comparison operator don't need to be correlated queries, but they can be. In the "Subqueries that retrieve rows satisfying a condition" section, we give examples of how a noncorrelated subquery can be used with the IN predicate. To show how a correlated subquery may use the IN predicate, ask the same question that came up with the EXISTS predicate: What are the names and phone numbers of the contacts at all of Penguin's customers in New Hampshire? You can answer this question with a correlated IN subquery:

```
SELECT *
    FROM CONTACT
    WHERE 'NH' IN
        (SELECT State
            FROM CUSTOMER
            WHERE CONTACT.CustomerID =
            CUSTOMER.CustomerID) ;
```

The statement is evaluated for each record in the CONTACT table. If, for that record, the CustomerID numbers in CONTACT and CUSTOMER match, the value of CUSTOMER.State is compared to 'NH'. The result of the subquery is a list that contains, at most, one element. If that one element is 'NH', the WHERE clause of the enclosing statement is satisfied, and a row is added to the query's result table.

Introducing a correlated subquery with a comparison operator

A correlated subquery can also be introduced by one of the six comparison operators, as shown in the next example.

Penguin pays bonuses to its salespeople based on their total monthly sales volume. The higher the volume, the higher the bonus percentage. The bonus percentage list is kept in the BONUSRATE table:

MinAmount	MaxAmount	BonusPct
0.00	24999.99	0.
25000.00	49999.99	0.01
50000.00	99999.99	0.02
100000.00	249999.99	0.03
250000.00	499999.99	0.04
500000.00	749999.99	0.05
750000.00	999999.99	0.06

If a person's monthly sales total is between $100,000.00 and $249,999.99, the bonus is 3 percent of sales.

Sales are recorded in a transaction master table named TRANSMASTER, which is created as follows:

```
CREATE TABLE TRANSMASTER (
    TransID       INTEGER       PRIMARY KEY,
    CustID        INTEGER       FOREIGN KEY,
    EmpID         INTEGER       FOREIGN KEY,
    TransDate     DATE,
    NetAmount     NUMERIC,
    Freight       NUMERIC,
    Tax           NUMERIC,
    InvoiceTotal  NUMERIC) ;
```

Sales bonuses are based on the sum of the NetAmount field for all of a person's transactions in the month. You can find any person's bonus rate with a correlated subquery that uses comparison operators:

```
SELECT BonusPct
    FROM BONUSRATE
        WHERE MinAmount <=
            (SELECT SUM(NetAmount)
                FROM TRANSMASTER
                    WHERE EmpID = 133)
            AND MaxAmount >=
                (SELECT SUM(NetAmount)
```

```
                 FROM TRANSMASTER
                 WHERE EmpID = 133) ;
```

This query is interesting in that it contains two subqueries, making use of the logical connective AND. The subqueries use the SUM aggregate operator, which returns a single value: the total monthly sales of employee 133. That value is then compared against the MinAmount and the MaxAmount columns in the BONUSRATE table, producing the bonus rate for that employee.

If you hadn't known the EmpID but had known the person's name, you could arrive at the same answer with a more complex query:

```
SELECT BonusPct
    FROM BONUSRATE
        WHERE MinAmount <=
            (SELECT SUM(NetAmount)
                FROM TRANSMASTER
                    WHERE EmpID =
                        (SELECT EmployeeID
                            FROM EMPLOYEE
                                WHERE EmplName =
                                    'Thornton'))
        AND MaxAmount >=
            (SELECT SUM(NetAmount)
                FROM TRANSMASTER
                    WHERE EmpID =
                        (SELECT EmployeeID
                            FROM EMPLOYEE
                                Where EmplName =
                                    'Thornton')) ;
```

This example uses subqueries nested within subqueries, which in turn are nested within an enclosing query, to arrive at the bonus rate for the employee named Thornton. This structure works only if you know for sure that the company has one, and only one, employee whose name is Thornton. If you know that more than one employee is named Thornton, you can add terms to the WHERE clause of the innermost subquery until you're sure that only one row of the EMPLOYEE table is selected.

Using correlated subqueries in a HAVING clause

You can have a correlated subquery in a HAVING clause just as you can in a WHERE clause. As we mention in Chapter 5, a HAVING clause is normally preceded by a GROUP BY clause. The HAVING clause acts as a filter to restrict the groups created by the GROUP BY clause. Groups that don't satisfy the condition of the HAVING clause are not included in the result. When used in this way, the HAVING clause is evaluated for each group created by the GROUP BY clause. In the absence of a GROUP BY clause, the HAVING clause is evaluated for the set of rows passed by the WHERE clause, which is considered to be a single group. If neither a WHERE clause nor a GROUP BY clause is present, the HAVING clause is evaluated for the entire table:

```
SELECT TM1.EmpID
    FROM TRANSMASTER TM1
        GROUP BY TM1.EmpID
        HAVING MAX(TM1.NetAmount) >= ALL
            (SELECT 2 * AVG (TM2.NetAmount)
            FROM TRANSMASTER TM2
            WHERE TM1.EmpID <> TM2.EmpID) ;
```

This query uses two aliases for the same table, enabling you to retrieve the EmpID number of all salespeople who had a sale of at least twice the average value of all the other salespeople. Short aliases such as TM1 are often used to eliminate excessive typing when long table names such as TRANSMASTER are involved. But in this case, aliases do more than just save some typing. The TRANSMASTER table is used for two different purposes, so two different aliases are used to distinguish between them. The query works as follows:

1. The outer query groups TRANSMASTER rows by the EmpID. This is done with the SELECT, FROM, and GROUP BY clauses.

2. The HAVING clause filters these groups. For each group, it calculates the MAX of the NetAmount column for the rows in that group.

3. The inner query evaluates twice the average NetAmount from all rows of TRANSMASTER whose EmpID is different from the EmpID of the current group of the outer query. Each group contains the transaction records for an employee whose

biggest sale had at least twice the value of the average of the sales of all the other employees. Note that in the last line, you need to reference two different EmpID values, so in the FROM clauses of the outer and inner queries, you use different aliases for TRANSMASTER.

4. You then use those aliases in the comparison of the query's last line to indicate that you're referencing both the EmpID from the current row of the inner subquery (TM2.EmpID) and the EmpID from the current group of the outer subquery (TM1.EmpID).

Using Subqueries in INSERT, DELETE, and UPDATE Statements

In addition to SELECT statements, UPDATE, DELETE, and INSERT statements can also include WHERE clauses. Those WHERE clauses can contain subqueries in the same way that SELECT statement WHERE clauses do.

For example, Penguin has just made a volume purchase deal with Baker Electronic Sales and wants to retroactively provide Baker with a 10 percent credit for all its purchases in the last month. You can give this credit with an UPDATE statement:

```
UPDATE TRANSMASTER
   SET NetAmount = NetAmount * 0.9
   WHERE CustID =
     (SELECT CustID
        FROM CUSTOMER
        WHERE Company = 'Baker
   Electronic Sales') ;
```

The subquery in an UPDATE statement WHERE clause operates the same as it does in a SELECT statement WHERE clause. The same is true for DELETE and INSERT. To delete all of Baker's transactions, use this statement:

```
DELETE FROM TRANSMASTER
   WHERE CustID =
     (SELECT CustomerID
        FROM CUSTOMER
```

```
            WHERE Company = 'Baker
    Electronic Sales') ;
```

As with UPDATE, DELETE subqueries can also be correlated and can also reference the table whose rows are being deleted. The rules are similar to the rules for UPDATE subqueries. Suppose you want to delete all rows from TRANSMASTER for customers whose total NetAmount is larger than $10,000:

```
DELETE FROM TRANSMASTER TM1
    WHERE 10000 < (SELECT SUM(NetAmount)
        FROM TRANSMASTER TM2
            WHERE TM1.CustID = TM2.CustID) ;
```

This query deletes all rows from TRANSMASTER referencing customers with purchases exceeding $10,000 — including the aforementioned customer with CustID 37. All references to TRANSMASTER in the subquery denote the contents of TRANSMASTER before any deletes by the current statement. So, even when you're deleting the last TRANSMASTER row, the subquery is evaluated on the original TRANSMASTER table, identified by TM1.

INSERT can include a SELECT clause. One use for this statement is filling *snapshot tables* (tables that take a snapshot of another table at a particular moment in time). For example, to create a table with the contents of TRANSMASTER for October 27, do this:

```
CREATE TABLE TRANSMASTER_1027
    (TransID INTEGER, TransDate DATE,
    ...) ;
INSERT INTO TRANSMASTER_1027
    (SELECT * FROM TRANSMASTER
        WHERE TransDate = 2018-10-27) ;
```

The CREATE TABLE statement creates an empty table; the INSERT INTO statement fills it with the data that was added on October 27. Or you may want to save rows only for large NetAmounts:

```
INSERT INTO TRANSMASTER_1027
    (SELECT * FROM TRANSMASTER
        WHERE TRANSMASTER.NetAmount > 10000
            AND TransDate = 2018-10-27) ;
```

Chapter 7

Querying Multiple Tables with Relational Operators

I n Chapter 6, we show you how, by using nested queries, data can be drawn from multiple tables to answer a question that involves different ideas. Another way to collect information from multiple tables is to use the relational operators UNION, INTERSECT, EXCEPT, and JOIN. SQL's UNION, INTERSECT, and EXCEPT operators are modeled after the union, intersect, and except operators of relational algebra. Each one performs a very specific combining operation on the data in two or more tables. The JOIN operator, on the other hand, is considerably more flexible. A number of different joins exist, and each performs a somewhat different operation. Depending on what you want in terms of information retrieved from multiple tables, one or another of the joins or the other relational operators is likely to give it to you. In this chapter, we show you each of SQL's relational operators, cover how it works, and discuss what you can use it for.

UNION

The UNION operator is the SQL implementation of the union operator used in relational algebra. SQL's UNION operator enables you to draw information from two or more tables that have the same structure. *Same structure* means

>> The tables must all have the same number of columns.

>> Corresponding columns must all have identical data types and lengths.

When these criteria are met, the tables are *union-compatible*. The union of two tables returns all the rows that appear in either table and eliminates duplicates.

Suppose you've created a database for a business named Acme Systems that sells and installs computer products. Acme has two warehouses that stock the products, one in Fort Deposit, Alabama, and the other in East Kingston, New Hampshire. It contains two union-compatible tables, named DEPOSIT and KINGSTON. Both tables have two columns, and corresponding columns are of the same type. In fact, corresponding columns have identical column names (although this condition isn't required for union compatibility).

DEPOSIT lists the names and quantity in stock of products in the Fort Deposit warehouse. KINGSTON lists the same information about the East Kingston warehouse. The UNION of the two tables gives you a virtual result table containing all the rows in the first table plus all the rows in the second table. For this example, we put just a few rows in each table to illustrate the operation:

```
SELECT * FROM DEPOSIT ;

ProductName        QuantityInStock
-----------        ---------------
185_Express               12
505_Express                5
510_Express                6
520_Express                2
550_Express                3
```

```
SELECT * FROM KINGSTON ;

ProductName       QuantityInStock
-----------       ----------------

185_Express              15
505_Express               7
510_Express               6
520_Express               2
550_Express               1


SELECT * FROM DEPOSIT
UNION
SELECT * FROM KINGSTON ;

ProductName       QuantityInStock
-----------       ----------------

185_Express              12
185_Express              15
505_Express               5
505_Express               7
510_Express               6
520_Express               2
550_Express               3
550_Express               1
```

The UNION DISTINCT operator functions identically to the UNION operator without the DISTINCT keyword. In both cases, duplicate rows are eliminated from the result set. In this example, because both warehouses had the same number of 510_Express and 520_Express products, those rows in both tables were exact duplicates, only one of which was returned.

This example shows how UNION works, but it isn't very practical. In most cases, Acme's manager probably wouldn't care which products were stocked in exactly the same numbers at both warehouses and, thus, partially removed from the result set. All the information is present, but the user must be savvy enough to realize that the total number of units of 510_Express is actually 12 rather than 6, and the total number of units of 520_Express is 4 rather than 2.

We use the asterisk (*) as shorthand for all the columns in a table. This shortcut is fine most of the time, but it can get you into trouble when you use relational operators in embedded or module-language SQL. What if you add one or more new columns to one table and not to another, or you add different columns to the two tables? The two tables are then no longer union compatible, and your program is invalid the next time it's recompiled. Even if the same new columns are added to both tables so that they're still union-compatible, your program is probably not prepared to deal with this additional data. So, explicitly listing the columns that you want rather than relying on the * shorthand is generally a good idea. When you're entering ad hoc SQL from the console, the asterisk will probably work fine because you can quickly display table structure to verify union compatibility if your query isn't successful.

UNION ALL

As we mention earlier, the UNION operation normally eliminates any duplicate rows that result from its operation, which is the desired result most of the time. Sometimes, however, you may want to preserve duplicate rows. On those occasions, use UNION ALL.

The following code shows you what UNION ALL produces when it's used with the DEPOSIT and KINGSTON tables:

```
SELECT * FROM DEPOSIT
UNION ALL
SELECT * FROM KINGSTON ;

ProductName          QuantityInStock
-----------          ---------------
185_Express               12
505_Express                5
510_Express                6
520_Express                2
550_Express                3
185_Express               15
505_Express                7
510_Express                6
520_Express                2
550_Express                1
```

UNION CORRESPONDING

You can sometimes form the union of two tables even if they aren't union compatible. If the columns you want in your result set are present and compatible in both source tables, you can perform a UNION CORRESPONDING operation. Only the specified columns are considered, and they're the only columns displayed in the result set.

Suppose Acme Systems opens a third warehouse, in Jefferson, Maine. A new table named JEFFERSON is added to the database, which includes Product and QuantityInStock columns (as the DEPOSIT and KINGSTON tables do), but also has an additional column named QuantityOnHold. A UNION or UNION ALL of JEFFERSON with either DEPOSIT or KINGSTON wouldn't return any rows because there isn't a complete match between all the columns of JEFFERSON and all the columns of the other two tables. However, you can still add the JEFFERSON data to that of either DEPOSIT or KINGSTON by specifying only the columns in JEFFERSON that correspond with the columns in the other table. Here's a sample query:

```
SELECT *
    FROM JEFFERSON
UNION CORRESPONDING BY
    (ProductName, QuantityInStock)
SELECT *
    FROM KINGSTON ;
```

The result table holds the products and the quantities in stock at both warehouses. As with the simple UNION, duplicates are eliminated. Thus, if the Jefferson warehouse happens to have the same quantity of a particular product that the Kingston warehouse has, the UNION CORRESPONDING operation loses one of those rows. To avoid this problem, use UNION ALL CORRESPONDING.

TIP

Each column name in the list following the CORRESPONDING keyword must be a name that exists in both unioned tables. If you omit this list of names, an implicit list of all names that appear in both tables is used. But this implicit list of names may change when new columns are added to one or both tables. Therefore, explicitly listing the column names is better than omitting them.

INTERSECT

The UNION operation produces a result table containing all rows that appear in at least one of the source tables. If you want only rows that appear in all the source tables, you can use the INTERSECT operation, which is the SQL implementation of relational algebra's intersect operation. We illustrate INTERSECT by returning to the Acme Systems warehouse table:

```
SELECT * FROM DEPOSIT ;

ProductName          QuantityInStock
-----------          ---------------

185_Express                12
505_Express                 5
510_Express                 6
520_Express                 2
550_Express                 3


SELECT * FROM KINGSTON ;

ProductName          QuantityInStock
-----------          ---------------

185_Express                15
505_Express                 7
510_Express                 6
520_Express                 2
550_Express                 1
```

Only rows that appear in all source tables show up in the INTERSECT operation's result table:

```
SELECT *
    FROM DEPOSIT
INTERSECT
SELECT *
    FROM KINGSTON;

ProductName          QuantityInStock
-----------          ---------------

510_Express                 6
520_Express                 2
```

The result table shows that the Fort Deposit and East Kingston warehouses both have exactly the same number of 510_Express and 520_Express products in stock, a fact of dubious value. Note that, as was the case with UNION, INTERSECT DISTINCT produces the same result as the INTERSECT operator used alone. In this example, only one of the identical rows displaying each of two products is returned.

The ALL and CORRESPONDING keywords function in an INTERSECT operation the same way they do in a UNION operation. If you use ALL, duplicates are retained in the result table. If you use CORRESPONDING, the intersected tables need not be union compatible, although the corresponding columns need to have matching types and lengths.

Consider another example: A municipality keeps track of the phones carried by police officers, firefighters, parking enforcement officers, and other city employees. A database table called PHONES contains data on all phones in active use. Another table named OUT, with an identical structure, contains data on all phones that have been taken out of service. No cellphone should ever exist in both tables. With an INTERSECT operation, you can test to see whether such an unwanted duplication has occurred:

```
SELECT *
    FROM PHONES
INTERSECT CORRESPONDING BY (PhoneID)
SELECT *
    FROM OUT ;
```

If the result table contains any rows, you know you have a problem. You should investigate any PhoneID entries that appear in the result table. The corresponding phone is either active or out of service; it can't be both. After you detect the problem, you can perform a DELETE operation on one of the two tables to restore database integrity.

EXCEPT

The UNION operation acts on two source tables and returns all rows that appear in *either* table. The INTERSECT operation returns all rows that appear in *both* the first and the second table.

In contrast, the EXCEPT (or EXCEPT DISTINCT) operation returns all rows that appear in the first table but that do *not* also appear in the second table.

Returning to the municipal phone database example, say that a group of phones that had been declared out of service and returned to the vendor for repairs have now been fixed and placed back into service. The PHONES table was updated to reflect the returned phones, but the returned phones were not removed from the OUT table as they should have been. You can display the PhoneID numbers of the phones in the OUT table, with the reactivated ones eliminated, using an EXCEPT operation:

```
SELECT *
   FROM OUT
EXCEPT CORRESPONDING BY (PhoneID)
SELECT *
   FROM PHONES;
```

This query returns all the rows in the OUT table whose PhoneID is not also present in the PHONES table. These are the phones still out of service.

JOINS

The UNION, INTERSECT, and EXCEPT operators are valuable in multitable databases in which the tables are union compatible. In many cases, however, you want to draw data from multiple tables that have very little in common. JOINs are powerful relational operators that combine data from multiple tables into a single result table. The source tables may have little (or even nothing) in common with each other.

SQL supports a number of types of JOINs. The best one to choose in a given situation depends on the result you're trying to achieve.

Cartesian product or cross join

Any multitable query is a type of JOIN. The source tables are joined in the sense that the result table includes information taken from all the source tables. The simplest JOIN is a two-table SELECT that has no WHERE clause qualifiers. Every row of the first table is joined to every row of the second table. The result table is referred to as the *Cartesian product* of the two source tables — the direct product of the two sets. (The less fancy name for the same thing is *cross join*.) The number of rows in the result table is equal to the number of rows in the first source table multiplied by the number of rows in the second source table.

For example, imagine that you're the personnel manager for a company, and that part of your job is to maintain employee records. Most employee data, such as home address and telephone number, is not particularly sensitive. But some data, such as current salary, should be available only to authorized personnel. To maintain security of the sensitive information, you'd probably keep it in a separate table that is password protected. Consider the following pair of tables:

```
EMPLOYEE                        COMPENSATION
--------                        ------------
EmpID                           Employ
FName                           Salary
LName                           Bonus
City
Phone
```

Fill the tables with some sample data:

EmpID	FName	LName	City	Phone
1	Jenny	Smith	Orange	555-1001
2	Bill	Jones	Newark	555-3221
3	Val	Brown	Nutley	555-6905
4	Jus	Time	Passaic	555-8908

Employ	Salary	Bonus
1	63000	10000
2	48000	2000
3	54000	5000
4	52000	7000

Create a virtual result table with the following query:

```
SELECT *
  FROM EMPLOYEE, COMPENSATION ;
```

which can also be written

```
SELECT *
  FROM EMPLOYEE CROSS JOIN COMPENSATION ;
```

Both of these formulations do exactly the same thing. This query produces the following:

EmpID	FName	LName	City	Phone	Employ	Salary	Bonus
1	Jenny	Smith	Orange	555-1001	1	63000	10000
1	Jenny	Smith	Orange	555-1001	2	48000	2000
1	Jenny	Smith	Orange	555-1001	3	54000	5000
1	Jenny	Smith	Orange	555-1001	4	52000	7000
2	Bill	Jones	Newark	555-3221	1	63000	10000
2	Bill	Jones	Newark	555-3221	2	48000	2000
2	Bill	Jones	Newark	555-3221	3	54000	5000
2	Bill	Jones	Newark	555-3221	4	52000	7000
3	Val	Brown	Nutley	555-6905	1	63000	10000
3	Val	Brown	Nutley	555-6905	2	48000	2000
3	Val	Brown	Nutley	555-6905	3	54000	5000
3	Val	Brown	Nutley	555-6905	4	52000	7000
4	Jus	Time	Passaic	555-8908	1	63000	10000
4	Jus	Time	Passaic	555-8908	2	48000	2000
4	Jus	Time	Passaic	555-8908	3	54000	5000
4	Jus	Time	Passaic	555-8908	4	52000	7000

The result table, which is the Cartesian product of the EMPLOYEE and COMPENSATION tables, contains considerable redundancy. Furthermore, it doesn't make much sense. It combines every row of EMPLOYEE with every row of COMPENSATION. The only rows that convey meaningful information are those in which the EmpID number that came from EMPLOYEE matches the Employ number that came from COMPENSATION. In those rows, an employee's name and address are associated with that same employee's compensation.

When you're trying to get useful information out of a multitable database, the Cartesian product produced by a cross join is almost never what you want, but it's almost always the first step toward what you want. By applying constraints to the JOIN with a WHERE clause, you can filter out the unwanted rows. The most common JOIN that uses the WHERE clause filter is the equi-join.

Equi-join

An *equi-join* is a cross join with the addition of a WHERE clause containing a condition specifying that the value in one column in the first table must be equal to the value of a corresponding column in the second table. Applying an equi-join to the example tables from the previous section brings a more meaningful result:

```
SELECT *
   FROM EMPLOYEE, COMPENSATION
   WHERE EMPLOYEE.EmpID = COMPENSATION.Employ ;
```

This produces the following:

EmpID	FName	LName	City	Phone	Employ	Salary	Bonus
1	Jenny	Smith	Orange	555-1001	1	63000	10000
2	Bill	Jones	Newark	555-3221	2	48000	2000
3	Val	Brown	Nutley	555-6905	3	54000	5000
4	Jus	Time	Passaic	555-8908	4	52000	7000

In this result table, the salaries and bonuses on the right apply to the employees named on the left. The table still has some redundancy because the EmpID column duplicates the Employ column. You can fix this problem by specifying in your query which columns you want selected from the COMPENSATION table:

```
SELECT EMPLOYEE.*,COMPENSATION.
   Salary,COMPENSATION.Bonus
   FROM EMPLOYEE, COMPENSATION
   WHERE EMPLOYEE.EmpID = COMPENSATION.Employ ;
```

This produces the following result:

EmpID	FName	LName	City	Phone	Salary	Bonus
1	Jenny	Smith	Orange	555-1001	63000	10000
2	Bill	Jones	Newark	555-3221	48000	2000
3	Val	Brown	Nutley	555-6905	54000	5000
4	Justin	Time	Passaic	555-8908	52000	7000

This table tells you what you want to know, but doesn't burden you with any extraneous data. The query is somewhat tedious to write, however. To avoid ambiguity, it makes sense to qualify the column names with the names of the tables they came from. However, writing those table names repeatedly can be tiresome.

You can cut down on the amount of typing by using aliases (or *correlation names*). An *alias* is a short name that stands for a table name. If you use aliases in recasting the preceding query, it comes out like this:

```
SELECT E.*, C.Salary, C.Bonus
    FROM EMPLOYEE E, COMPENSATION C
    WHERE E.EmpID = C.Employ ;
```

In this example, E is the alias for EMPLOYEE, and C is the alias for COMPENSATION. The alias is local to the statement it's in. After you declare an alias (in the FROM clause), you must use it throughout the statement. You can't use both the alias and the long form of the table name.

Mixing the long form of table names with aliases creates confusion. Consider the following example, which is confusing:

```
SELECT T1.C, T2.C
    FROM T1 T2, T2 T1
    WHERE T1.C > T2.C ;
```

In this example, the alias for T1 is T2, and the alias for T2 is T1. Admittedly, this isn't a smart selection of aliases, but it isn't forbidden by the rules. If you mix aliases with long-form table names, you can't tell which table is which.

The preceding example with aliases is equivalent to the following SELECT with no aliases:

```
SELECT T2.C, T1.C
  FROM T1, T2
  WHERE T2.C > T1.C ;
```

SQL enables you to join more than two tables. The maximum number varies from one implementation to another. The syntax is analogous to the two-table case:

```
SELECT E.*, C.Salary, C.Bonus, Y.TotalSales
  FROM EMPLOYEE E, COMPENSATION C, YTD_SALES Y
  WHERE E.EmpID = C.Employ
    AND C.Employ = Y.EmpNo ;
```

This statement performs an equi-join on three tables, pulling data from corresponding rows of each one to produce a result table that shows the salespeople's names, the amount of sales they're responsible for, and their compensation. The sales manager can quickly see whether compensation is in line with production.

TIP

Storing a salesperson's year-to-date sales in a separate YTD_SALES table ensures better performance and reliability than keeping that data in the EMPLOYEE table. The data in the EMPLOYEE table is relatively static. A person's name, address, and telephone number don't change very often. In contrast, the year-to-date sales change frequently (you hope). Because the YTD_SALES table has fewer columns than EMPLOYEE, you may be able to update it more quickly. If, in the course of updating sales totals, you don't touch the EMPLOYEE table, you decrease the risk of accidentally modifying EMPLOYEE information that should stay the same.

Natural join

The *natural join* is a special case of an equi-join. In the WHERE clause of an equi-join, a column from one source table is compared with a column of a second source table for equality. The two columns must be the same type and length and must have the same name. In fact, in a natural join, *all* columns in one table that have the same names, types, and lengths as corresponding columns in the second table are compared for equality.

Imagine that the COMPENSATION table from the preceding example has columns EmpID, Salary, and Bonus rather than Employ, Salary, and Bonus. In that case, you can perform a natural join of the COMPENSATION table with the EMPLOYEE table. The traditional JOIN syntax looks like this:

```
SELECT E.*, C.Salary, C.Bonus
    FROM EMPLOYEE E, COMPENSATION C
    WHERE E.EmpID = C.EmpID ;
```

This query is a natural join. An alternate syntax for the same operation is the following:

```
SELECT E.*, C.Salary, C.Bonus
    FROM EMPLOYEE E NATURAL JOIN COMPENSATION C ;
```

Condition join

A *condition join* is like an equi-join, except the condition being tested doesn't have to be equality (although it can be). It can be any well-formed predicate. If the condition is satisfied, the corresponding row becomes part of the result table. The syntax is a little different from what you've seen so far, in that the condition is contained in an ON clause rather than a WHERE clause.

Suppose Acme Systems wants to know which products the Fort Deposit warehouse has in larger numbers than does the East Kingston warehouse. This question is a job for a condition join:

```
SELECT *
    FROM DEPOSIT JOIN KINGSTON
    ON DEPOSIT.QuantityInStock >
        KINGSTON.QuantityInStock ;
```

Within the predicate of a condition join, ON syntax is used in place of WHERE syntax.

Column-name join

The *column-name join* is like a natural join, but it's more flexible. In a natural join, all the source table columns that have the same name are compared with each other for equality. With the column-name join, you select which same-name columns to compare.

You can choose them all if you want, making the column-name join effectively a natural join. Or you may choose fewer than all same-name columns. In this way, you have a great degree of control over which cross product rows qualify to be placed into your result table.

Suppose you're Acme Systems, and you've shipped the exact same number of products to the East Kingston warehouse that you've shipped to the Fort Deposit warehouse. So far, nothing has been sold, so the number of products in inventory in East Kingston should match the number in Fort Deposit. If there are mismatches, it means that something is wrong. Either some products were never delivered to the warehouse, or they were misplaced or stolen after they arrived. With a simple query, you can retrieve the inventory levels at the two warehouses.

```
SELECT * FROM DEPOSIT ;

ProductName          QuantityInStock
-----------          ---------------
185_Express               12
505_Express                5
510_Express                6
520_Express                2
550_Express                3

SELECT * FROM KINGSTON ;

ProductName          QuantityInStock
-----------          ---------------
185_Express               15
505_Express                7
510_Express                6
520_Express                2
550_Express                1
```

For such small tables, it's fairly easy to see which rows don't match. However, for a table with thousands of rows, it's not so easy. You can use a column-name join to see whether any discrepancies exist. We show only two columns of the DEPOSIT and KINGSTON tables to make it easy to see how the various relational operators work on them. In any real application, though, such tables would have additional columns, and the contents of those additional columns wouldn't necessarily match. With a column-name join, the join operation considers only the columns specified.

```
SELECT *
    FROM DEPOSIT JOIN KINGSTON
    USING (ProductName, QuantityInStock) ;
```

Note the USING keyword, which tells the relational database management system (RDBMS) which columns to use.

The result table shows only the rows for which the number of products in stock at Fort Deposit equals the number of products in stock at East Kingston:

ProdName	QuantInStock	ProdName	QuantInStock
510_Express	6	510_Express	6
520_Express	2	520_Express	2

Wow! Only two products match. There is a definite "shrinkage" problem at one or both warehouses. Acme needs to get a handle on security.

Inner join

By now, you're probably getting the idea that joins are pretty esoteric and that it takes an uncommon level of spiritual discernment to deal with them adequately. You may have even heard of the mysterious *inner join* and speculated that it probably represents the core or essence of relational operations. Well, ha! The joke is on you: There's nothing mysterious about inner joins. In fact, all the joins covered so far in this chapter are inner joins. We could've formulated the column-name join in the last example as an inner join by using the following syntax:

```
SELECT *
    FROM DEPOSIT INNER JOIN KINGSTON
    USING (ProductName, QuantityInStock) ;
```

The result is the same.

The inner join is so named to distinguish it from the outer join. An *inner join* discards all rows from the result table that don't have corresponding rows in both source tables. An *outer join* preserves unmatched rows. That's the difference. Nothing metaphysical about it.

Outer join

When you're joining two tables, the first one (call it the one on the left) may have rows that don't have matching counterparts in the second table (the one on the right). Conversely, the table on the right may have rows that don't have matching counterparts in the table on the left. If you perform an inner join on those tables, all the unmatched rows are excluded from the output. *Outer joins*, however, don't exclude the unmatched rows. Outer joins come in three types: the left outer join, the right outer join, and the full outer join.

Left outer join

In a query that includes a join, the left table is the one that precedes the keyword JOIN and the right table is the one that follows it. The *left outer join* preserves unmatched rows from the left table but discards unmatched rows from the right table.

To understand outer joins, consider a corporate database that maintains records of the company's employees, departments, and locations. Tables 7-1, 7-2, and 7-3 contain the database's sample data.

TABLE 7-1 LOCATION

LocationID	CITY
1	Boston
3	Tampa
5	Chicago

TABLE 7-2 **DEPT**

DeptID	LocationID	NAME
21	1	Sales
24	1	Admin
27	5	Repair
29	5	Stock

TABLE 7-3 **EMPLOYEE**

EmpID	DeptID	NAME
61	24	Kirk
63	27	McCoy

Now suppose that you want to see all the data for all employees, including department and location. You get this with an equi-join:

```
SELECT *
    FROM LOCATION L, DEPT D, EMPLOYEE E
    WHERE L.LocationID = D.LocationID
        AND D.DeptID = E.DeptID ;
```

This statement produces the following result:

```
1    Boston    24    1    Admin     61    24    Kirk
5    Chicago   27    5    Repair    63    27    McCoy
```

This results table gives all the data for all the employees, including their location and department. The equi-join works because every employee has a location and a department.

Suppose now that you want the data on the locations, with the related department and employee data. This is a different problem because a location without any associated departments may exist. To get what you want, you have to use an outer join, as in the following example:

```
SELECT *
    FROM LOCATION L LEFT OUTER JOIN DEPT D
        ON (L.LocationID = D.LocationID)
    LEFT OUTER JOIN EMPLOYEE E
        ON (D.DeptID = E.DeptID);
```

This join pulls data from three tables. First, the LOCATION table is joined to the DEPT table. The resulting table is then joined to the EMPLOYEE table. Rows from the table on the left of the LEFT OUTER JOIN operator that have no corresponding row in the table on the right are included in the result. Thus, in the first join, all locations are included, even if no department associated with them exists. In the second join, all departments are included, even if no employee associated with them exists. The result is as follows:

1	Boston	24	1	Admin	61	24	Kirk
5	Chicago	27	5	Repair	63	27	McCoy
3	Tampa	NULL	NULL	NULL	NULL	NULL	NULL
5	Chicago	29	5	Stock	NULL	NULL	NULL
1	Boston	21	1	Sales	NULL	NULL	NULL

The first two rows are the same as the two result rows in the previous example. The third row (3 Tampa) has nulls in the department and employee columns because no departments are defined for Tampa and no employees are stationed there. (Perhaps Tampa is a brand-new location and it hasn't yet been staffed.) The fourth and fifth rows (5 Chicago and 1 Boston) contain data about the Stock and the Sales departments, but the employee columns for these rows contain nulls because these two departments have no employees. This outer join tells you everything that the equi-join told you plus the following:

>> All the company's locations, whether or not they have any departments

>> All the company's departments, whether or not they have any employees

The rows returned in the preceding example aren't guaranteed to be in the order you want. The order may vary from one implementation to the next. To make sure that the rows returned are in the order you want, add an ORDER BY clause to your SELECT statement, like this:

```
SELECT *
    FROM LOCATION L LEFT OUTER JOIN DEPT D
        ON (L.LocationID = D.LocationID)
    LEFT OUTER JOIN EMPLOYEE E
        ON (D.DeptID = E.DeptID)
    ORDER BY L.LocationID, D.DeptID, E.EmpID;
```

TIP

You can abbreviate the left outer join language as LEFT JOIN because there's no such thing as a left inner join.

Right outer join

By now, you've probably figured out how the right outer join behaves. It preserves unmatched rows from the right table but discards unmatched rows from the left table. You can use it on the same tables and get the same result by reversing the order in which you present tables to the join:

```
SELECT *
    FROM EMPLOYEE E RIGHT OUTER JOIN DEPT D
        ON (D.DeptID = E.DeptID)
    RIGHT OUTER JOIN LOCATION L
        ON (L.LocationID = D.LocationID) ;
```

In this formulation, the first join produces a table that contains all departments, whether they have an associated employee or not. The second join produces a table that contains all locations, whether they have an associated department or not.

TIP

You can abbreviate the right outer join language as RIGHT JOIN because there's no such thing as a right inner join.

Full outer join

The *full outer join* combines the functions of the left outer join and the right outer join. It retains the unmatched rows from both the left and the right tables. Consider the most general case of the company database used in the preceding examples. It could have

>> Locations with no departments

>> Locations with no employees

- » Departments with no locations
- » Departments with no employees
- » Employees with no locations
- » Employees with no departments

REMEMBER

Whereas the preceding named conditions are unusual, they can happen, particularly in a startup situation, and when they do, you'll be glad you have outer joins to deal with them. As soon as you say that a certain situation isn't possible, reality will conk you on the head with an example of that very situation.

To show all locations, departments, and employees, regardless of whether they have corresponding rows in the other tables, use a full outer join in the following form:

```
SELECT *
    FROM LOCATION L FULL OUTER JOIN DEPT D
        ON (L.LocationID = D.LocationID)
    FULL OUTER JOIN EMPLOYEE E
        ON (D.DeptID = E.DeptID) ;
```

TIP

You can abbreviate the full outer join language as FULL JOIN because there's no such thing as a full inner join.

ON versus WHERE

The function of the ON and WHERE clauses in the various types of joins is potentially confusing. These facts may help you keep things straight:

- » The ON clause is part of the inner, left, right, and full joins. The cross join and UNION join don't have an ON clause because neither of them does any filtering of the data.

- » The ON clause in an inner join is logically equivalent to a WHERE clause; the same condition could be specified either in the ON clause or in a WHERE clause.

- » The ON clauses in outer joins (left, right, and full joins) are different from WHERE clauses. The WHERE clause simply filters the rows returned by the FROM clause. Rows rejected by the filter aren't included in the result. The ON clause in an outer join first filters the rows of a cross product and then includes the rejected rows, extended with nulls.

Join Conditions and Clustering Indexes

The performance of queries that include joins depends, to a large extent, on which columns are indexed, and whether the index is clustering or not. A table can have only one clustering index, where data items that are near each other logically, such as 'Smith' and 'Smithson', are also near each other physically on disk. Using a clustering index to sequentially step through a table speeds up hard disk retrievals and, thus, maximizes performance.

REMEMBER

An index is a separate table that corresponds to a data table, but is sorted in some order. A clustering index is an index sorted in the same order that items are stored in memory and, thus, provides the fastest retrievals.

A clustering index works well with multipoint queries, which look for equality in nonunique columns. This is similar to looking up names in a telephone book. All the Smiths are listed together on consecutive pages. Most or all of them are located on the same hard disk cylinder. You can access multiple Smiths with a single disk seek operation. A nonclustering index, on the other hand, would not have this advantage. Each record typically requires a new disk seek, greatly slowing down operation. Furthermore, you probably have to touch every index to be sure you haven't missed one.

Consider the following sample query:

```
SELECT Employee.FirstName, Employee.LastName,
    Student.Major
    FROM Employee, Students
    WHERE Employee.IDNum = Student.IDNum ;
```

This query returns the first and last names and the majors of university employees who are also students. How long it takes to run the query depends on how the tables are indexed. If Employee has a clustering index on IDNum, records searched are on consecutive pages. If Employee and Student both have cluster-ing indexes on IDNum, the RDBMS will likely use a merge join, which reads both tables in sorted order, minimizing the number of disk accesses needed. Such clustering often eliminates the need for a costly ORDER BY clause because the records are already sorted in the desired order.

The one disadvantage of clustered indexes is that they can become "tired" after a number of updates have been performed, caus-ing the generation of overflow pages, which require additional disk seeks. Rebuilding the index corrects this problem. By tired, we mean "less helpful." Every time you add or delete a record, the index loses some of its advantage. A deleted record must be skipped over, and added records must be put on an overflow page, which will usually require a couple of extra disk seeks.

Some modern RDBMS products perform automatic clustered index maintenance, meaning they rebuild clustered indexes with-out having to be told to do so. If you have such a product, then the disadvantage that we just noted goes away.

Chapter **8**
Cursors

SQL differs from most other computer languages in one important respect: Other languages — such as C, Java, and Basic — are *procedural languages* because programs written in those languages set out a specified series of operations that need to be carried out in the same manner and in the same order — *procedures,* in other words. That means procedural languages first execute one instruction, and then the next one, then the next, and so on. The pertinent point here is that they can do only one thing at a time, so when they're asked to deal with data, they operate on one table row at a time. SQL is a *nonprocedural language,* so it isn't restricted to operating on a single table row at a time. Its natural mode of operation is to operate on a set of rows. For example, an SQL query may return 42 rows from a database containing thousands of rows. That operation is performed by a single SQL SELECT statement.

REMEMBER

Because SQL is a data sublanguage, it does not contain all the features needed to create a database application. It must be used in combination with a procedural language. The SQL portion operates on the data, and the procedural language takes care of the other aspects of the task.

The fact that SQL normally operates on data a set at a time rather than a row at a time constitutes a major incompatibility between SQL and the most popular application development languages.

A *cursor* enables SQL to retrieve (or update, or delete) a single row at a time so that you can use SQL in combination with an application written in any of the procedural languages.

REMEMBER

A cursor is like a pointer that locates a specific table row. When a cursor is active, you can SELECT, UPDATE, or DELETE the row at which the cursor is pointing.

Cursors are valuable if you want to retrieve selected rows from a table, check their contents, and perform different operations based on those contents. SQL can't perform this sequence of operations by itself. SQL can retrieve the rows, but procedural languages are better at making decisions based on field contents. Cursors enable SQL to retrieve rows from a table one at a time and then feed the result to procedural code for processing. By placing the SQL code in a loop, you can process the entire table row by row.

In a pseudocode representation of how embedded SQL meshes with procedural code, the most common flow of execution looks like this:

```
EXEC SQL DECLARE CURSOR statement
EXEC SQL OPEN statement
Test for end of table
Procedural code
Start loop
    Procedural code
    EXEC SQL FETCH
    Procedural code
    Test for end of table
End loop
EXEC SQL CLOSE statement
Procedural code
```

The SQL statements in this listing are DECLARE, OPEN, FETCH, and CLOSE. Each of these statements is discussed in detail in this chapter.

TIP

If you can perform the operation that you want with normal SQL statements — which operate on data one set at a time — do so. Declare a cursor, retrieve table rows one at a time, and use your system's host language only when normal SQL can't do what you want.

Declaring a Cursor

To use a cursor, you first must declare its existence to the relational database management system (RDBMS). You do this with a DECLARE CURSOR statement. The DECLARE CURSOR statement doesn't actually cause anything to happen; it just announces the cursor's name to the RDBMS and specifies what query the cursor will operate on. A DECLARE CURSOR statement has the following syntax:

```
DECLARE cursor-name [cursor sensitivity]
  [cursor scrollability]
CURSOR [cursor holdability]
    [cursor returnability]
FOR query expression
    [ORDER BY order-by expression]
    [FOR updatability expression] ;
```

Note: The cursor name uniquely identifies a cursor, so it must be unlike that of any other cursor name in the current module or compilation unit.

TIP

To make your application more readable, give the cursor a meaningful name. Relate it to the data that the query expression requests or to the operation that your procedural code performs on the data.

Cursor sensitivity may be SENSITIVE, INSENSITIVE, or ASENSITIVE. Cursor scrollability may be either SCROLL or NO SCROLL. Cursor holdability may be either WITH HOLD or WITHOUT HOLD. Cursor returnability may be either WITH RETURN or WITHOUT RETURN. All these terms are explained in the following sections.

The query expression

REMEMBER

The *query expression* can be any legal SELECT statement. The rows that the SELECT statement retrieves are the ones that the cursor steps through one at a time. These rows are the scope of the cursor.

The query is not actually performed when the DECLARE CURSOR statement given in the previous pseudocode is read. You can't retrieve data until you execute the OPEN statement. The row-by-row examination of the data starts after you enter the loop that encloses the FETCH statement.

Ordering the query result set

You may want to process your retrieved data in a particular order, depending on what your procedural code does with the data. You can sort the retrieved rows before processing them by using the optional ORDER BY clause. The clause has the following syntax:

```
ORDER BY sort-specification
    [ , sort-specification]...
```

You can have multiple sort specifications. Each has the following syntax:

```
(column-name) [COLLATE BY collation-name ]
    [ASC|DESC]
```

You sort by column name, and to do so, the column must be in the select list of the query expression. Columns that are in the table but not in the query select list do not work as sort specifications. For example, say you want to perform an operation that is not supported by SQL on selected rows of the CUSTOMER table. You can use a DECLARE CURSOR statement like this:

```
DECLARE cust1 CURSOR FOR
    SELECT CustID, FirstName, LastName,
        City, State, Phone
    FROM CUSTOMER
    ORDER BY State, LastName, FirstName ;
```

In this example, the SELECT statement retrieves rows sorted first by state, then by last name, and then by first name. The statement retrieves all customers in New Jersey (NJ) before it retrieves the first customer from New York (NY). The statement then sorts customer records from Alaska by the customer's last name (*Aaron* before *Abbott)*. Where the last name is the same, sorting then goes by first name (*George Aaron* before *Henry Aaron).*

Have you ever made 40 copies of a 20-page document on a photocopier without a collator? What a drag! You have to make 20 stacks on tables and desks, and then walk by the stacks 40 times, placing a sheet on each stack. This process is called *collation*. A similar process plays a role in SQL.

A *collation* is a set of rules that determines how strings in a character set compare. A character set has a default collation sequence that defines the order in which elements are sorted. But you can apply a collation sequence other than the default to a column. To do so, use the optional COLLATE BY clause. Your implementation probably supports several common collations. Pick one and then make the collation ascending or descending by appending an ASC or DESC keyword to the clause.

In a DECLARE CURSOR statement, you can specify a calculated column that doesn't exist in the underlying table. In this case, the calculated column doesn't have a name that you can use in the ORDER BY clause. You can give it a name in the DECLARE CURSOR query expression, which enables you to identify the column later. Consider the following example:

```
DECLARE revenue CURSOR FOR
    SELECT Model, Units, Price,
           Units * Price AS ExtPrice
        FROM TRANSDETAIL
    ORDER BY Model, ExtPrice DESC ;
```

In this example, no COLLATE BY clause is in the ORDER BY clause, so the default collation sequence is used. Notice that the fourth column in the select list comes from a calculation on the data in the second and third columns. The fourth column is an extended price named ExtPrice. In the ORDER BY clause, we first sort by model name and then by ExtPrice. The sort on ExtPrice is descending, as specified by the DESC keyword; transactions with the highest dollar value are processed first.

REMEMBER

The default sort order in an ORDER BY clause is ascending. If a sort specification list includes a DESC sort and the next sort should also be in descending order, you must explicitly specify DESC for the next sort. For example:

```
ORDER BY A, B DESC, C, D, E, F
```

is equivalent to

```
ORDER BY A ASC, B DESC, C ASC, D ASC, E ASC, F ASC
```

Updating table rows

Sometimes, you may want to update or delete table rows that you access with a cursor. Other times, you may want to guarantee that such updates or deletions can't be made. SQL gives you control over this issue with the updatability clause of the DECLARE CURSOR statement. If you want to prevent updates and deletions within the scope of the cursor, use this clause:

```
FOR READ ONLY
```

For updates of specified columns only — leaving all others protected — use the following:

```
FOR UPDATE OF column-name [ , column-name]...
```

REMEMBER

Any columns listed must appear in the DECLARE CURSOR's query expression. If you don't include an updatability clause, the default assumption is that all columns listed in the query expression are updatable. In that case, an UPDATE statement can update all the columns in the row to which the cursor is pointing, and a DELETE statement can delete that row.

Sensitive versus insensitive cursors

The query expression in the DECLARE CURSOR statement determines the rows that fall within a cursor's scope. Consider this possible problem: What if a statement in your program, located between the OPEN and CLOSE statements, changes the contents of some of those rows so that they no longer satisfy the query? What if such a statement deletes some of those rows entirely? Does the cursor continue to process all the rows that originally qualified, or does it recognize the new situation and ignore rows that no longer qualify or that have been deleted?

REMEMBER

Changing the data in columns that are part of a DECLARE CURSOR query expression after some — but not all — of the query's rows have been processed results in a big mess. Your results are likely to be inconsistent and misleading. To avoid this problem, make your cursor insensitive to any changes that statements within its scope may make. Add the INSENSITIVE keyword to your DECLARE CURSOR statement. As long as your cursor is open, it is insensitive to table changes that otherwise affect rows qualified to be included in the cursor's scope. A cursor can't be both insensitive and updatable. An insensitive cursor must be read-only.

Think of it this way: A normal SQL statement, such as UPDATE, INSERT, or DELETE, operates on a set of rows in a database table (perhaps the entire table). While such a statement is active, SQL's transaction mechanism protects it from interference by other statements acting concurrently on the same data. If you use a cursor, however, your window of vulnerability to harmful interaction is wide open. When you open a cursor, you're at risk until you close it again. If you open one cursor, start processing through a table, and then open a second cursor while the first is still active, the actions you take with the second cursor can affect what the statement controlled by the first cursor sees. For example, suppose that you write these queries:

```
DECLARE C1 CURSOR FOR SELECT * FROM EMPLOYEE
   ORDER BY Salary ;
DECLARE C2 CURSOR FOR SELECT * FROM EMPLOYEE
   FOR UPDATE OF Salary ;
```

Now, suppose you open both cursors and fetch a few rows with C1 and then update a salary with C2 to increase its value. This change can cause a row that you've already fetched with C1 to appear again on a later fetch that uses C1.

The peculiar interactions possible with multiple open cursors, or open cursors and set operations, are the sort of concurrency problems that transaction isolation avoids. If you operate this way, you're asking for trouble. If you have multiple open cursors, that means that you're performing more than one operation at a time. If those concurrent operations happen to interact with each other, you may get unpredictable results. This is similar to the kind of harmful interaction that enclosing your operations within a transaction protects you from. The difference is that using transactions protects you from harmful interference by other users. Having only one cursor open at a time protects you from harmful interactions with yourself. So, remember: Don't operate with multiple open cursors.

The default condition of cursor sensitivity is ASENSITIVE. The meaning of ASENSITIVE is implementation dependent. For one implementation, it could be equivalent to SENSITIVE and, for another, it could be equivalent to INSENSITIVE. Check your system documentation for its meaning in your own case.

Scrolling a cursor

Scrollability is a capability that cursors didn't have prior to SQL-92. In implementations adhering to SQL-86 or SQL-89, the only allowed cursor movement was sequential, starting at the first row retrieved by the query expression and ending with the last row. SQL-92's SCROLL keyword in the DECLARE CURSOR statement gives you the capability to access rows in any order you want. The current version of SQL retains this capability. The syntax of the FETCH statement controls the cursor's movement. We describe the FETCH statement later in this chapter (see the "Operating on a Single Row" section).

Holding a cursor

Earlier, we mention that a cursor could be declared either WITH HOLD or WITHOUT HOLD (you're probably wondering what *that's* all about), that it's a bad idea to have more than one cursor open at a time, and that transactions are a mechanism for preventing two users from interfering with each other. All these ideas are interrelated.

In general, it's a good idea to enclose any database operation consisting of multiple SQL statements in a transaction. This is fine most of the time, but whenever a transaction is active, the resources it uses are off-limits to all other users. Furthermore, results are not saved to permanent storage until the transaction is closed. For a very lengthy transaction, where a cursor is stepping through a large table, it may be beneficial to close the transaction in order to flush results to disk, and then reopen it to continue processing. The problem with this is that the cursor will lose its place in the table. To avoid this problem, use the WITH HOLD syntax. When WITH HOLD is declared, the cursor won't be automatically closed when the transaction closes — it'll be left open. When the new transaction is opened, the still open cursor can pick up where it left off and continue processing. WITHOUT HOLD is the default condition, so if you don't mention HOLD in your cursor declaration, the cursor closes automatically when the transaction that encloses it is closed.

Declaring a result set cursor

A procedure invoked from another procedure or function may need to return a result set to the invoking procedure or function. If this is the case, the cursor must be declared with the WITH RETURN syntax. The default condition is WITHOUT RETURN.

Opening a Cursor

Although the DECLARE CURSOR statement specifies which rows to include in the cursor, it doesn't actually cause anything to happen because DECLARE is a declaration and not an executable statement. The OPEN statement brings the cursor into existence. It has the following form:

```
OPEN cursor-name ;
```

To open the cursor that we use in the discussion of the ORDER BY clause (earlier in this chapter), use the following:

```
DECLARE revenue CURSOR FOR
    SELECT Model, Units, Price,
           Units * Price AS ExtPrice
        FROM TRANSDETAIL
    ORDER BY Model, ExtPrice DESC ;
OPEN revenue ;
```

REMEMBER

You can't fetch rows from a cursor until you open the cursor. When you open a cursor, the values of variables referenced in the DECLARE CURSOR statement become fixed, as do all current date-time functions. Consider the following example of SQL statements embedded in a host language program:

```
EXEC SQL DECLARE CURSOR C1 FOR SELECT *
    FROM ORDERS
            WHERE ORDERS.Customer = :NAME
            AND DueDate < CURRENT_DATE ;
NAME := 'Acme Co';       //A host language statement
EXEC SQL OPEN C1;
NAME := 'Omega Inc.';   //Another host statement
...
EXEC SQL UPDATE ORDERS SET DueDate = CURRENT_DATE;
```

The OPEN statement fixes the value of all variables referenced in the DECLARE CURSOR statement and also fixes a value for all current datetime functions. Thus, the second assignment to the name variable (NAME := 'Omega Inc.') has no effect on the rows that the cursor fetches. (That value of NAME is used the next time you open C1.) And even if the OPEN statement is executed a minute before midnight and the UPDATE statement is executed a minute after midnight, the value of CURRENT_DATE in the UPDATE statement is the value of that function at the time the OPEN statement executed. This is true even if DECLARE CURSOR doesn't reference the datetime function.

Operating on a Single Row

Whereas the DECLARE CURSOR statement specifies the cursor's name and scope, and the OPEN statement collects the table rows selected by the DECLARE CURSOR query expression, the FETCH statement actually retrieves the data. The cursor may point to one of the rows in the cursor's scope, or to the location immediately before the first row in the scope, or to the location immediately after the last row in the scope, or to the empty space between two rows. You can specify where the cursor points with the orientation clause in the FETCH statement.

FETCH syntax

The syntax for the FETCH statement is

```
FETCH [[orientation] FROM] cursor-name
    INTO target-specification [, target-
    specification]... ;
```

Seven orientation options are available:

>> NEXT

>> PRIOR

>> FIRST

>> LAST

>> ABSOLUTE

>> RELATIVE

>> <simple value specification>.

The default option is NEXT, which was the only orientation available in versions of SQL prior to SQL-92. It moves the cursor from wherever it is to the next row in the set specified by the query expression. If the cursor is located before the first record, it moves to the first record. If it points to record n, it moves to record n + 1. If the cursor points to the last record in the set, it moves beyond that record, and notification of a no data condition is returned in the SQLSTATE system variable.

The target specifications are either host variables or parameters, respectively, depending on whether embedded SQL or module language is using the cursor. The number and types of the target specifications must match the number and types of the columns specified by the query expression in the DECLARE CURSOR statement. So, in the case of embedded SQL, when you fetch a list of five values from a row of a table, five host variables must be there to receive those values, and they must be the right types.

Absolute versus relative fetches

Because the SQL cursor is scrollable, you have other choices besides NEXT. If you specify PRIOR, the pointer moves to the row immediately preceding its current location. If you specify FIRST, it points to the first record in the set, and if you specify LAST, it points to the last record.

An integer value specification must accompany ABSOLUTE and RELATIVE. For example, FETCH ABSOLUTE 7 moves the cursor to the seventh row from the beginning of the set. FETCH RELATIVE 7 moves the cursor seven rows beyond its current position. FETCH RELATIVE 0 doesn't move the cursor.

FETCH RELATIVE 1 has the same effect as FETCH NEXT. FETCH RELATIVE -1 has the same effect as FETCH PRIOR. FETCH ABSOLUTE 1 gives you the first record in the set, FETCH ABSOLUTE 2 gives you the second record in the set, and so on. Similarly, FETCH ABSOLUTE -1 gives you the last record in the set, FETCH ABSOLUTE -2 gives you the next-to-last record, and so on. Specifying FETCH ABSOLUTE 0 returns the no data exception condition code, as does FETCH ABSOLUTE 17 if only 16 rows are in the set. FETCH <simple value specification> gives you the record specified by the simple value specification.

Deleting a row

You can perform delete and update operations on the row that the cursor is currently pointing to. The syntax of the DELETE statement is as follows:

```
DELETE FROM tablename WHERE CURRENT OF
    cursorname ;
```

If the cursor doesn't point to a row, the statement returns an error condition. No deletion occurs.

Updating a row

The syntax of the UPDATE statement is as follows:

```
UPDATE tablename
    SET columnname = value [,columnname = value]...
    WHERE CURRENT OF cursorname ;
```

The value you place into each specified column must be a value expression or the keyword DEFAULT. If an attempted positioned update operation returns an error, the update isn't performed. (A *positioned* update operation, as distinct from an ordinary set-oriented update operation, is an update of the row the cursor is currently pointing to.)

Closing a Cursor

TIP

After you finish with a cursor, make a habit of closing it immediately. Leaving a cursor open as your application goes on to other issues may cause harm. Someone may open another cursor on the same table, and you may forget it's open and perform an operation that you don't intend to. Also, open cursors use system resources.

If you close a cursor that was insensitive to changes made while it was open, when you reopen it, the reopened cursor reflects any such changes.

The syntax for closing cursor C1 is:

```
CLOSE C1 ;
```

IN THIS CHAPTER

» Controlling operations with SQL

» Identifying users and specifying roles

» Categorizing users

» Granting and revoking privileges

» Granting and revoking roles

Chapter 9

Assigning Access Privileges

B ecause databases are among the most valuable assets that any organization has, you must be able to control who has access to them, as well as what level of access to grant. SQL handles access management with the third of its main components, the Data Control Language (DCL). Whereas the Data Definition Language (DDL) is used to create and maintain the structure of a database and the Data Manipulation Language (DML) is used to fill the database structure with data and then operate on that data, the DCL protects the database from unauthorized access and other potential problems.

Working with the SQL Data Control Language

The DCL consists of four SQL statements, and two of them — COMMIT and ROLLBACK — control how the database handles query transactions. The other two DCL statements — GRANT and REVOKE — control who may access various parts of the database. Before you can grant database access to someone, you must have some way of identifying that person. Some parts of user identification, such as issuing passwords and taking other security measures, are implementation specific. SQL has a standard way of identifying and categorizing users, however, so granting and revoking privileges can be handled relatively easily.

Identifying Authorized Users

Users may be identified individually with a unique identifier, or they may be identified as a member of a group. Individually identified users can be given a customized array of access privileges, whereas all group members receive the same suite of privileges. Groups are defined by the roles that the people in them play. People who all perform the same role have the same access privileges.

Understanding user identifiers

SQL doesn't specify how a user identifier is assigned. In many cases, the operating system's login ID serves the purpose. A user identifier is one of two forms of authorization identifier that enable access to a database system. The other form is a role name, which we discuss in the next section.

Every SQL session is started by a user. That user's user identifier is called the *SQL-session user identifier*. The privileges associated with the SQL-session user identifier determine what privileges that user has and what actions they may perform during the session. When your SQL session starts, your SQL-session user identifier is also the *current user identifier*. The identity of the current user is kept in a special value named CURRENT_USER, which can be queried to find out who is currently in charge of a session.

Getting familiar with roles

In a small company, identifying users individually doesn't present any problem. In a larger organization, however, with hundreds of employees doing a variety of jobs, identifying users individually can become a burden. Every time someone leaves or joins a company or changes job responsibilities, database privileges have to be adjusted. This adjustment is where roles come in.

Although a company may have hundreds or thousands of employees, these employees do a limited number of jobs. If everyone who plays the same role in the company requires the same database access privileges, you can assign those privileges to that group of people based on the roles they play in the organization. One role may be SALES_CLERK. All the sales clerks require the same privileges. All the warehouse workers require different privileges, which is fine, because they play a different role in the company. In this way, the job of maintaining authorizations for everyone is made much simpler. A new sales clerk is added to the SALES_CLERK role name and immediately gains the privileges assigned to that role. A sales clerk leaving the company is deleted from the SALES_CLERK role name and immediately loses all database privileges. An employee changing from one job category to another is deleted from one role name and added to another.

Just as a session initiated by a user is associated with an SQL-session user identifier, it's also associated with an SQL-session role name. The value of the current role name is available in the CURRENT_ROLE special value. When an SQL session is created, the current role name has a null value. At any given instant, either a user identifier is specified and the associated role name has a null value, or a role name is specified and the associated user identifier has a null value. A SET ROLE statement can create a situation in which both the user identifier for a session and a role name are non-null. In such a case, the privileges assigned to both the user identifier and the role name are available to the user.

Creating roles

You can create a role with a single SQL statement. Here's the syntax:

```
CREATE ROLE rolename
    [WITH ADMIN {CURRENT_USER | CURRENT_ROLE}] ;
```

When you create a role, the role is automatically granted to you. You're also granted the right to pass the role-creation privilege on to others. When creating a role, you may identify yourself as either the current user or the current role. If you identify yourself as the current user, you're the only one who can operate on the new role. If you identify yourself as the current role, anyone who shares your current role is also able to operate on the new role.

Destroying roles

The syntax for destroying a role is easy to understand:

```
DROP ROLE rolename ;
```

Classifying Users

Aside from the fact that users may be members of a group identified as a role, there are four classes of users. Each of these classes has associated privileges that may supersede the privileges accorded to a user by virtue of their role. The four classes are as follows:

>> **Database administrator (DBA):** Every database has at least one DBA and possibly multiple DBAs. It's the responsibility of the DBA to maintain the database, making sure that it's protected from harm and operating at peak efficiency. DBAs have full rights to all the objects in the database. They can create, modify, or destroy any object in the database, including tables and indexes. They can also decide what privileges other users may have.

>> **Database object owners:** Users who create database objects such as tables and views are automatically the owners of those objects. A database object owner possesses all privileges related to that object. A database object owner's privileges are equal to those of a DBA, but only with respect to the object in question.

>> **Grantees:** *Grantees* are users who have been granted selected privileges by a DBA or database object owner. A grantee may or may not be given the right to grant their privileges to others, who, thus, also become grantees.

>> **The public:** All users are considered to be part of the public, regardless of whether they've been specifically granted any privileges. Thus, privileges granted to PUBLIC may be exercised by any user.

Granting Privileges

The GRANT statement is the tool you use to grant privileges to users. A fairly large number of privileges may be granted, and they may apply to a fairly large number of objects. As a result, the syntax of the GRANT statement is lengthy. Don't let the length intimidate you! The syntax is very logical and fairly simple when you become familiar with it. Here's the syntax:

```
GRANT privilegelist
  ON privilegeobject
  TO userlist [WITH GRANT OPTION]
  [GRANTED BY {CURRENT_USER | CURRENT_ROLE}] ;
<privilege list> ::= privilege [ , privilege]...

<privilege> ::=
    SELECT [(columnname [ , columnname]...)]
  | SELECT (methoddesignator [ ,
      methoddesignator]...)
  | DELETE
  | INSERT [(columnname [ , columnname]...)]
  | UPDATE [(columnname [ , columnname]...)]
  | REFERENCES [(columnname [ ,
      columnname]...)]
  | USAGE
  | TRIGGER
  | UNDER
  | EXECUTE

<privilege object> ::=
    [TABLE] tablename
  | viewname
  | DOMAIN domainname
  | CHARACTER SET charactersetname
  | COLLATION collationname
  | TRANSLATION translationname
  | TYPE user-definedtypename
  | specificroutinedesignator
```

```
userlist ::=
    authorizationID [ , authorizationID]...
    | PUBLIC
```

Whew! That's a lot of syntax. Look at it piece-by-piece so that it's a little more comprehensible.

Not all privileges apply to all privilege objects. The SELECT, DELETE, INSERT, UPDATE, and REFERENCES privileges apply to the TABLE PRIVILEGE object. The SELECT privilege also applies to views. The USAGE privilege applies to the DOMAIN, CHARACTER SET, COLLATION, and TRANSLATION objects. The TRIGGER privilege applies, logically enough, to triggers. The UNDER privilege applies to user-defined types, and the EXECUTE privilege applies to specific routines.

Looking at data

The first privilege in the privilege list is the privilege of looking at a database object. The SELECT statement retrieves data from database tables and views. To enable a user to execute the SELECT statement, issue a GRANT SELECT statement, like this example:

```
GRANT SELECT
   ON CUSTOMER
   TO SALES_MANAGER ;
```

This statement enables the sales manager to query the CUSTOMER table.

Deleting data

In a similar fashion, the GRANT DELETE statement enables a user to delete specified rows from a table, as follows:

```
GRANT DELETE
   ON CUSTOMER
   TO SALES_MANAGER ;
```

This statement enables the sales manager to prune inactive customers from the customer table.

Adding data

With the INSERT statement, you can add a new row of data to a table. The GRANT INSERT statement determines who has the right to perform this operation, as follows:

```
GRANT INSERT
  ON CUSTOMER
  TO SALES_MANAGER ;
```

Now the sales manager can add a new customer record to the CUSTOMER table.

Changing data

You can change the contents of a table row with the UPDATE statement. GRANT UPDATE determines who can do it, as in this example:

```
GRANT UPDATE
  ON RETAIL_PRICE_LIST
  TO SALES_MANAGER ;
```

Now the sales manager can update the retail price list with new pricing information.

Using certain database facilities

The USAGE privilege applies to domains and user-defined types (UDTs). We've talked about domains before; UDTs are exactly what the name implies, data types that users have defined. We describe them in the "Defining new data types" section, later in this chapter. To use or even see a domain or UDT, a user must have the USAGE privilege for that domain or UDT. Suppose that Major League Baseball has a domain named MLBTEAMS that consists of the names of all the Major League Baseball teams. A user holding the role of team owner could be granted use of that domain, as follows:

```
GRANT USAGE
  ON MLBTEAMS
  TO TEAM_OWNER ;
```

Responding to an event

You can grant a user or a role the privilege of creating a trigger that fires when a specified change takes place to a table, such as the renaming of a Major League Baseball team, as in this example:

```
GRANT TRIGGER
    ON MLBTEAMS
    TO TEAM_OWNER ;
```

Defining new data types

One advanced feature that was added to SQL in the SQL:1999 version enables users to create structured user-defined types. Naturally, the creator of a UDT has all privileges attached to that UDT. Among those privileges is the USAGE privilege, which allows the type to be used to define columns, routines, and other schema objects. Also included is the UNDER privilege, which permits sub-types of the type to be defined, as follows:

```
GRANT UNDER
    ON MLBTEAMS
    TO LEAGUE_VICE_PRESIDENT ;
```

Executing an SQL statement

The EXECUTE privilege enables the grantee to use SQL-invoked routines. By restricting the ability to invoke routines, you keep those routines in the hands of those who are authorized to run them, as in this example:

```
GRANT EXECUTE
    ON PRICECHANGE
    TO SALES_MANAGER ;
```

Doing it all

For a highly trusted person who has just been given major responsibility, instead of issuing a whole series of GRANT statements, you can take care of everything with just one statement, GRANT ALL. Here's an example:

```
GRANT ALL PRIVILEGES
    ON MLBTEAMS
    TO LEAGUE_VICE_PRESIDENT ;
```

GRANT ALL PRIVILEGES is a pretty dangerous statement, however. In the wrong hands, it could cause a lot of damage. For this reason, SQL Server 2005 deprecated this syntax.

Passing on the power

To keep your system secure, you must severely restrict the access privileges you grant and the people to whom you grant these privileges. People who can't do their work because they lack access, however, are likely to hassle you. To preserve your sanity, you probably need to delegate some of the responsibility for maintaining database security.

SQL provides for such delegation through the WITH GRANT OPTION clause. Consider the following example:

```
GRANT UPDATE
    ON RETAIL_PRICE_LIST
    TO SALES_MANAGER WITH GRANT OPTION ;
```

This statement is similar to the GRANT UPDATE example (refer to "Changing data," earlier in this chapter) in that the statement enables the sales manager to update the retail price list. The statement also gives them the right to grant the update privilege to anyone they want. If you use this form of the GRANT statement, you must not only trust the grantee to use the privilege wisely, but also trust them to choose wisely in granting the privilege to others.

Revoking Privileges

If it's possible to grant database privileges to users and roles, it had better be possible to revoke those privileges, too. Things change. People's jobs change, and their need for data changes. Sometimes people leave the company and go to work for a competitor. You certainly want to revoke privileges in a case like that.

The syntax for revoking privileges is similar to the GRANT syntax, as follows:

```
REVOKE [GRANT OPTION FOR] privilegelist
    ON privilegeobject
    FROM user list
    [GRANTED BY {CURRENT_USER | CURRENT_ROLE}]
    {RESTRICT | CASCADE} ;
```

The privilege list, privilege object, and user list are the same as they are for GRANT. The major difference from the GRANT syntax is the addition of the RESTRICT and CASCADE keywords. Note that {RESTRICT | CASCADE} isn't enclosed in square brackets, meaning that it isn't optional. One of the two keywords is required in any REVOKE statement.

REMEMBER

In SQL Server's T-SQL, the CASCADE keyword *is* optional, and the RESTRICT sense is assumed if CASCADE is not present.

If a REVOKE statement includes the RESTRICT keyword, the RDBMS checks to see whether the privilege being revoked was passed on to one or more other users. If it was, the privilege isn't revoked, and you receive an error message instead. If a REVOKE statement includes the CASCADE keyword, the RDBMS revokes the privilege, as well as any dependent instances of this privilege that were granted by the instance you're revoking.

With the optional GRANT OPTION FOR clause, you can revoke a user's ability to grant a privilege without revoking their ability to use the privilege themselves. If you specify GRANT OPTION FOR along with CASCADE, not only is the grant option taken away, but also, everyone who obtained the privilege through that grant loses the privilege. If you specify GRANT OPTION FOR along with RESTRICT, and anyone was granted the privilege under consideration, you get an error message, and the grant option isn't revoked.

If the optional GRANTED BY clause is present, only those privileges granted by the current user or current role (whichever is specified) are revoked.

If none of the privileges you're trying to revoke exists, you get an error message and nothing changes. If some of the privileges you're trying to revoke exist, but others don't, you get a warning.

REMEMBER

Revoking a user's privileges may not remove those privileges from the user. If you granted the SELECT privilege to Alice WITH GRANT OPTION, and Alice granted the privilege to Bob, Bob has the SELECT privilege. If you later grant the SELECT privilege to Bob, now he has that privilege from two sources. If you revoke the SELECT privilege from Bob, he still has SELECT access to the table in question because of the GRANT SELECT he received from Alice. This situation complicates revocation. If you want to truly be sure that a person no longer has access to a resource, you must make sure that all grants have been revoked.

Granting Roles

Just as you can grant a privilege to a user, you can grant a role to a user. Granting a role is a more significant action: When you grant a role to a person, you're granting all the privileges that go along with that role in one action. Here's the syntax:

```
GRANT <role name> [{ , rolename}...]
    TO userlist
    [WITH ADMIN OPTION]
    [GRANTED BY {CURRENT_USER | CURRENT_ROLE}] ;
```

As you can see from the syntax, you can grant any number of roles to the names in a list of users with a single GRANT statement. The optional WITH ADMIN OPTION clause is similar to the WITH GRANT OPTION clause that may be a part of a grant of privileges. If you want to grant a role and extend to the grantee the right to grant the same role to others, you do so with the WITH ADMIN OPTION clause. The optional GRANTED BY clause specifies whether you want to record that this GRANT was granted by the current user or by the current role. This distinction may become meaningful when the time comes to revoke the role granted here.

Revoking Roles

The command for revoking a role is very similar to the command for revoking a privilege. Here's what it looks like:

```
REVOKE [ADMIN OPTION FOR] rolename
   [{ , rolename}...]
   FROM userlist
   [GRANTED BY {CURRENT_USER | CURRENT_ROLE}]
   {RESTRICT | CASCADE}
```

Here, you revoke one or more roles from the users in the user list. You can revoke the admin option from a role without revoking the role itself.

The GRANTED BY clause requires a little explanation. If a role was specified as being granted by the current user, revoking it with a GRANTED BY CURRENT_USER clause works, but revoking it with GRANTED BY CURRENT_ROLE clause doesn't. The RESTRICT or CASCADE keywords apply only if the admin option has been used to grant the specified role to other users or roles. If RESTRICT is specified and this role or list of roles has been granted to a subgrantee, an error message is returned and the revocation doesn't take effect. If CASCADE is specified and this role or list of roles has been granted to a subgrantee, the role and all the subgrantee roles are revoked.

Chapter **10**

Ten Retrieval Tips

A database can be a virtual treasure trove of information, but like the treasure of the Caribbean pirates of long ago, the stuff that you really want is probably buried and hidden from view. The SQL SELECT statement is your tool for digging up this hidden information. Even if you have a clear idea of what you want to retrieve, translating that idea into SQL can be a challenge. If your formulation is just a little off, you may end up with the wrong results — but results that are so close to what you expected that they mislead you. To reduce your chances of being misled, use the following ten tips.

Verify the Database Structure

If you retrieve data from a database and your results don't seem reasonable, check the database design. Many poorly designed databases are in use, and if you're working with one, fix the design before you try any other remedy. *Remember:* Good design is a prerequisite of data integrity.

Try Queries on a Test Database

Create a test database that has the same structure as your production database, but with only a few representative rows in the tables. Choose the data so you know in advance what the results of your queries should be. Run each test query on the test data, and see whether the results match your expectations. If they don't, you may need to reformulate your queries. If a query is properly formulated but you still end up with bad results, you may need to restructure your database.

Build several sets of test data and be sure to include odd cases, such as empty tables and extreme values at the very limit of allowable ranges. Try to think of unlikely scenarios and check for proper behavior when they occur. In the course of checking for unlikely cases, you may gain insight into problems that are more likely to happen.

Double-Check Queries That Include Joins

Joins are notoriously counterintuitive. If your query contains one, make sure that it's doing what you expect before you add WHERE clauses or other complicating factors.

Triple-Check Queries with Subselects

Queries with subselects take data from one table and, based on what's retrieved, take some data from another table. Therefore, by definition, such queries can really be hard to get right. Make sure the data that the inner SELECT retrieves is the data that the outer SELECT needs to produce the desired result. If you have two or more levels of subselects, you need to be even more careful.

Summarize Data with GROUP BY

Say that you have a table (NATIONAL) that contains the name (Player), team (Team), and number of home runs hit (Homers) by every baseball player in the National League. You can retrieve the team homer total for all teams with a query like this:

```
SELECT Team, SUM (Homers)
    FROM NATIONAL
    GROUP BY Team ;
```

This query lists each team, followed by the total number of home runs hit by all of that team's players.

Watch GROUP BY Clause Restrictions

Suppose you want a list of National League power hitters. Consider the following query:

```
SELECT Player, Team, Homers
    FROM NATIONAL
    WHERE Homers >= 20
    GROUP BY Team ;
```

In most implementations, this query returns an error. Generally, only columns used for grouping or columns used in a set function may appear in the select list. However, if you want to view this data, the following formulation works:

```
SELECT Player, Team, Homers
    FROM NATIONAL
    WHERE Homers >= 20
    GROUP BY Team, Player, Homers ;
```

Because all the columns you want to display appear in the GROUP BY clause, the query succeeds and delivers the desired results. This formulation sorts the resulting list first by Team, then by Player, and finally by Homers.

Use Parentheses with AND, OR, and NOT

Sometimes when you mix AND and OR, SQL doesn't process the expression in the order that you expect. Use parentheses in complex expressions to make sure that you get the desired results. Typing a few extra keystrokes is a small price to pay for better results.

Parentheses also help to ensure that the NOT keyword is applied to the term or expression that you want it to apply to.

Control Retrieval Privileges

Many people don't use the security features available in their relational database management system (RDBMS). They don't want to bother with security features because they think misuse and misappropriation of data are things that only happen to other people. Don't wait to get burned! Establish and maintain security for all databases that have any value.

Back Up Your Databases Regularly

Understatement alert: Data is hard to retrieve after a power surge, a fire, an earthquake, or some other disaster destroys your hard drive. (*Remember:* Sometimes computers just die for no good reason.) Make frequent backups, and put the backup media in a safe place.

What constitutes a safe place depends on how critical your data is. It may be a fireproof safe in the same room as your computer. It may be in another building. It may be in the cloud. It may be in a concrete bunker under a mountain that has been hardened to withstand a nuclear attack. Decide what level of safety is appropriate for your data.

Handle Error Conditions Gracefully

Whether you're making ad hoc queries from a workstation or embedding queries in an application, occasionally SQL returns an error message rather than the desired results. At a workstation, you can decide what to do next, based on the message returned. In an application, the situation is different. The application user probably doesn't know what action is appropriate. Put extensive error handling into your applications to cover every conceivable error that may occur. Creating error-handling code takes a great deal of effort, but it's better than having the user stare quizzically at a frozen screen.

Index

A

ABS function, 66
absolute fetches, 161
abstract data types (ADTs), 37
access privileges
  about, 163
  assigning, 163–174
  classifying users, 166
  granting privileges, 167–171
  granting roles, 173
  identifying authorized users, 164–166
  revoking privileges, 171–173
  revoking roles, 174
  working with SQL Data Control Language (DCL), 163–164
accessing SQL editor in Microsoft Access, 7–10
ACOS function, 66
actual cardinality, 73
adding data, 45–47, 169
adjusting
  data, 169
  table structure, 24–25
aggregate functions. *See* set functions
ALL predicate, 90–93
ALTER statement, 13
AND connective, 100, 177–178
ANY predicate, 90–93
ANY_VALUE function, 59
applying constraints, 38–43
approximate numerics, 30
Aristotle (philosopher), 90–91
ARRAY type, 35–36
array value expressions, 73
ASIN function, 66
assertions, 43
assigning access privileges, 163–174
asterisk (*), 44, 80, 130

ATAN function, 66
authorized users
  about, 164
  identifying, 164–166
  roles, 164–166
  user identifiers, 164
AVG function, 57–58

B

backing up databases, 178
BETWEEN predicate, 84–85
BIGINT type, 29, 52
BINARY LARGE OBJECT type, 32, 53
binary strings, 32
BINARY type, 32, 53
BINARY VARYING type, 32
blank space (' '), 61, 62
Boole, George (mathematician), 32
BOOLEAN type, 32–33
Boolean value expressions, 72–73
Booleans, 32–33
bypassing null values with COALESCE, 76–77

C

candidate key, 17
cardinality, 65–66, 73
CARDINALITY function, 65–66, 73
Cartesian product, 81, 134–137
CASCADE keyword, 172, 174
CASE expression, 74–76
cases, managing different, 74–76
CAST expression, converting data types with, 77–78
CEIL/CEILING function, 67
CHARACTER LARGE OBJECT type, 31, 53
character strings, 30–32
CHARACTER type, 31, 53

CHARACTER VARYING type, 31
CHARACTER_LENGTH function, 64
CHECK constraint, 40
classifying users, 166
CLOSE statement, 156
closing cursors, 162
clustering indexes, 148–149
COALESCE expression, bypassing null values with, 76–77
Codd's First Normal Form (1NF), 35
COLLATE BY clause, 155
collation, 155
collections, 35–36
column constraints
  about, 20, 38
  CHECK, 40
  NOT NULL, 38–39
  UNIQUE, 39
column references, entering, 52
column-name joins, 140–142
comma-separated values (CSVs), 58
comparison operators, 112, 121–123
comparison predicates
  BETWEEN, 84–85
  IN, 85–87
  about, 83–84
  ALL, 90–93
  ANY, 90–93
  AND connective, 100
  DISTINCT, 94
  EXISTS, 93
  LIKE, 87–89
  logical connectives, 99–101
  MATCH, 96–99
  NOT connective, 101
  NOT IN, 85–87
  NOT LIKE, 87–89
  NULL, 89–90
  OR connective, 101
  OVERLAPS, 95
  referential integrity, 97–99
  SOME, 90–93
  UNIQUE, 94

composite key, 17
concatenation operator (| |), 70
condition joins, 140, 148–149
conditional value expressions
  about, 74
  bypassing null values with
    COALESCE, 76–77
  managing different cases, 74–76
  NULLIF special CASE, 76
constraints
  applying, 38–43
  column, 38–40
  foreign key, 42
  setting, 20
  table, 40–41
constructor, 37–38
CONVERT function, 62
converting data types with CAST
  expression, 77–78
Coordinated Universal Time (UTC), 34, 71
correlated subqueries, 110, 119–125
correlation names, 138
COS function, 66
COSH function, 66
COUNT function, 57
create, read, update, and delete (CRUD), 7
CREATE DOMAIN statement, 21
CREATE statement, 13
CREATE TABLE statement, 14, 17–19, 126
creating
  databases with SQL, 13–25
  roles, 165
  tables, 14–19
cross joins, 134–137
current user identifier, 164
CURRENT_DATE function, 68–69
CURRENT_TIME function, 68–69
CURRENT_TIMESTAMP function, 68–69
CURRENT_USER variable, 55
cursors
  about, 151–152
  closing, 162
  declaring, 153–159
  declaring result set, 158

About the Authors

Richard Blum: Rich has worked in the IT industry for more than 35 years as a network and systems administrator. During that time, he has had the opportunity to work with lots of different operating systems, including IBM mainframes and Windows, Netware, UNIX, and Linux servers, as well as many different database systems such as Oracle, IBM Informix, Microsoft SQL Server, PostgreSQL, and MySQL. Over the years, he has also volunteered for several nonprofit organizations to help support small networks that had little financial support. Rich is the author of several Linux-based books for total Linux geeks and teaches online courses in programming. When he's not busy being a computer nerd, Rich enjoys playing piano and bass guitar, and spending time with his wife, Barbara, and their two daughters, Katie Jane and Jessica.

Allen G. Taylor: Allen is a 40-year veteran of the computer industry and the author of more than 40 books, including *SQL For Dummies, Crystal Reports 2008 For Dummies, Database Development For Dummies, Access 2003 Power Programming with VBA,* and *SQL Weekend Crash Course* (all published by Wiley). He lectures internationally on databases, networks, innovation, astronomy, and entrepreneurship, as well as health and wellness. He also teaches database development through a leading online education provider. For the latest news on Allen's activities, check out his online courses (at https://pioneer-academy1.teachable.com) and his blog (at www.allengtaylor.com). You can contact Allen at allen.taylor@ieee.org.

Dedication

This book is dedicated to the many teachers, authors, coworkers, friends, students, and online posters who have helped expand my computer knowledge over these many years.

"The way of a fool is right in his own eyes, but a wise man listens to advice." —Proverbs 12:15 (ESV)

—Richard Blum

Authors' Acknowledgments

From Richard Blum: First, all praise and glory go to God, who through His Son makes all things possible, and gives us the gift of eternal life.

A special thanks to Allen for his amazing and excellent work with the past editions of the *SQL For Dummies* series. It has been my pleasure to update the text to the latest SQL standards.

Many thanks go to the great people at John Wiley & Sons for their help and guidance in writing this book. Thanks to Lindsay Berg for offering me the opportunity to pick up this project. Also, many thanks to Elizabeth Kuball for helping keep the project focused and on track! Thanks also goes to Carole Jelen at Waterside Productions for arranging this gig and keeping my book-writing career on track.

Finally, I'd like to thank my parents, Mike and Joyce Blum, for constantly stressing education over goofing off, as well as my wife, Barbara, and two daughters, Katie Jane and Jessica, for their love and support, especially while I was working on this project

From Allen G. Taylor: First and foremost, I would like to acknowledge the help of Jim Melton, editor of the ISO/ANSI specification for SQL. Without his untiring efforts, this book — and, indeed, SQL itself as an international standard — would be of much less value. Thanks also to my agent, Carole McClendon of Waterside Productions, for her support of my career.

Publisher's Acknowledgments

Executive Editor: Lindsay Berg

Editor: Elizabeth Kuball

Proofreader: Debbye Butler

Production Editor:
Tamilmani Varadharaj

Cover Design and Image: Wiley

Leverage the power

Dummies is the global leader in the reference category and one of the most trusted and highly regarded brands in the world. No longer just focused on books, customers now have access to the dummies content they need in the format they want. Together we'll craft a solution that engages your customers, stands out from the competition, and helps you meet your goals.

Advertising & Sponsorships

Connect with an engaged audience on a powerful multimedia site, and position your message alongside expert how-to content. Dummies.com is a one-stop shop for free, online information and know-how curated by a team of experts.

- Targeted ads
- Video
- Email Marketing
- Microsites
- Sweepstakes sponsorship

20 MILLION
PAGE VIEWS
EVERY SINGLE MONTH

15 MILLION
UNIQUE
VISITORS PER MONTH

43%
OF ALL VISITORS
ACCESS THE SITE
VIA THEIR MOBILE DEVICES

700,000 NEWSLETTE
SUBSCRIPTION
TO THE INBOXES OF
300,000 UNIQUE INDIVIDUALS
EVERY WEEK

# of dummies

Custom Publishing

Reach a global audience in any language by creating a solution that will differentiate you from competitors, amplify your message, and encourage customers to make a buying decision.

- Apps
- Books
- eBooks
- Video
- Audio
- Webinars

Brand Licensing & Content

Leverage the strength of the world's most popular reference brand to reach new audiences and channels of distribution.

For more information, visit dummies.com/biz

PERSONAL ENRICHMENT

Staying Sharp

9781119187790
USA $26.00
CAN $31.99
UK £19.99

Facebook

9781119179030
USA $21.99
CAN $25.99
UK £16.99

Guitar

9781119293354
USA $24.99
CAN $29.99
UK £17.99

Investing

9781119293347
USA $22.99
CAN $27.99
UK £16.99

Beekeeping

9781119310068
USA $22.99
CAN $27.99
UK £16.99

Digital Photography

9781119235606
USA $24.99
CAN $29.99
UK £17.99

Meditation

9781119251163
USA $24.99
CAN $29.99
UK £17.99

Pregnancy

9781119235491
USA $26.99
CAN $31.99
UK £19.99

Samsung Galaxy S7

9781119279952
USA $24.99
CAN $29.99
UK £17.99

iPhone

9781119283133
USA $24.99
CAN $29.99
UK £17.99

Crocheting

9781119287117
USA $24.99
CAN $29.99
UK £16.99

Nutrition

9781119130246
USA $22.99
CAN $27.99
UK £16.99

PROFESSIONAL DEVELOPMENT

Windows 10

9781119311041
USA $24.99
CAN $29.99
UK £17.99

AutoCAD

9781119255796
USA $39.99
CAN $47.99
UK £27.99

Excel 2016

9781119293439
USA $26.99
CAN $31.99
UK £19.99

QuickBooks 2017

9781119281467
USA $26.99
CAN $31.99
UK £19.99

macOS Sierra

9781119280651
USA $29.99
CAN $35.99
UK £21.99

LinkedIn

9781119251132
USA $24.99
CAN $29.99
UK £17.99

Windows 10

9781119310563
USA $34.00
CAN $41.99
UK £24.99

SharePoint 2016

9781119181705
USA $29.99
CAN $35.99
UK £21.99

Fundamental Analysis

9781119263593
USA $26.99
CAN $31.99
UK £19.99

Networking

9781119257769
USA $29.99
CAN $35.99
UK £21.99

Office 2016

9781119293477
USA $26.99
CAN $31.99
UK £19.99

Office 365

9781119265313
USA $24.99
CAN $29.99
UK £17.99

Salesforce.com

9781119239314
USA $29.99
CAN $35.99
UK £21.99

Coding

9781119293323
USA $29.99
CAN $35.99
UK £21.99